Virtual Vic

Virtual Vic

A Management Fable

Laurence M. Rose, PhD

BEP | BUSINESS EXPERT PRESS

Virtual Vic: A Management Fable
Copyright © Business Expert Press, LLC, 2019.

All rights reserved. No part of this publication may be reproduced, stored in a retrieval system, or transmitted in any form or by any means—electronic, mechanical, photocopy, recording, or any—other except for brief quotations, not to exceed 250 words, without the prior permission of the publisher.

First published in 2019 by
Business Expert Press, LLC
222 East 46th Street, New York, NY 10017
www.businessexpertpress.com

ISBN-13: 978-1-94858-047-2 (paperback)
ISBN-13: 978-1-94858-048-9 (e-book)

Business Expert Press Human Resource Management and Organizational Behavior Collection

Collection ISSN: 1946-5637 (print)
Collection ISSN: 1946-5645 (electronic)

Cover and interior design by S4Carlisle Publishing Services Private Ltd., Chennai, India

First edition: 2019

10 9 8 7 6 5 4 3 2 1

Printed in the United States of America.

Virtual Vic

A Management Fable

Laurence M. Rose, PhD

BUSINESS EXPERT PRESS

Virtual Vic: A Management Fable
Copyright © Business Expert Press, LLC, 2019.

All rights reserved. No part of this publication may be reproduced, stored in a retrieval system, or transmitted in any form or by any means—electronic, mechanical, photocopy, recording, or any—other except for brief quotations, not to exceed 250 words, without the prior permission of the publisher.

First published in 2019 by
Business Expert Press, LLC
222 East 46th Street, New York, NY 10017
www.businessexpertpress.com

ISBN-13: 978-1-94858-047-2 (paperback)
ISBN-13: 978-1-94858-048-9 (e-book)

Business Expert Press Human Resource Management and Organizational Behavior Collection

Collection ISSN: 1946-5637 (print)
Collection ISSN: 1946-5645 (electronic)

Cover and interior design by S4Carlisle Publishing Services Private Ltd., Chennai, India

First edition: 2019

10 9 8 7 6 5 4 3 2 1

Printed in the United States of America.

Abstract

Virtual Vic is a management fable about the trials and tribulations of a new executive facing the virtual work environment and the technology associated with this environment. The story explores his struggles to be a successful leader by relying solely on technology and ignoring the human touch aspects behind true leadership. The story helps all of us look at technology as the tool it is meant to be rather than the humanistic hindrance it often becomes. Vic meets three characters (his informal Board of Directors) who help provide the lessons needed to best lead a blended workforce. Each character represents a major theme within the book. The themes of Trust (Reliable Reggie), Isolation (Solitary Samantha), and Presence (Being Bob) are about human perceptions that provide a human touch associated with the virtual work environment. Trust, isolation, and presence are the three main human perceptions discussed throughout the book.

Told in a fable style, *Virtual Vic* can help managers and employees recognize signs that could result in a less-than-ideal work environment. The book is designed for anyone associated with leading or managing teams especially those with the virtual work environment. The lessons discussed allow for the most productive workforce.

Keywords

board of director; human perceptions; isolation; leadership; management; presence; productivity; team; technology; TIP Scale; trust; virtual work environment

Contents

Preface .... *ix*
Acknowledgments .... *xi*
Introduction .... *xv*

Chapter 1	Virtual Vic 1
Chapter 2	Vic Meets Reliable Reggie 15
Chapter 3	Vic Meets Solitary Samantha...................................29
Chapter 4	Vic Meets Being Bob..47
Chapter 5	The Department Meeting...61
Chapter 6	Self-Efficacy 71
Chapter 7	Trust 73
Chapter 8	Isolation 75
Chapter 9	Presence 79
Chapter 10	Personal Touch...81

Endnotes *85*
About the Author...*87*
Index *89*

Preface

This book is the continuation of the theory and process I developed related to leading in the virtual work environment. My first book, *The Human Side of Virtual Work: Managing Trust Isolation, and Presence,* introduced the main character in this book, *Virtual Vic.* This book is written as a management fable that dives deeper into the challenges leaders face managing a blended workforce: colocated employees and virtual employees. It serves as a continuation of the theory and process of leading a blended workforce through the eyes of a fictitious executive leader. It is written to be a fun story that highlights the challenges faced and lessons learned by leaders in the virtual work environment. I continue to explore that humanistic management is a concept needed in managing and leading in the new organizational structure that affords companies who have virtual workers as part of their workforce..

The reason I chose to write using fictitious characters is to help illustrate the trials and tribulations of using technology while managing a workforce in the virtual work environment. I want to emphasis, within the story, what can happen when we remove the human touch. The story is designed to highlight areas of concern while leading a blended workforce. I also highlight the differences between leading colocated employees and virtual employees and how the same approaches might not work for all. The intent of this book is not to get heavy into the science behind theories and processes associated with leadership but rather to be an easy to read story. It highlights the lessons through telling the story from Vic's vision and approaches.

As virtual workers continue to populate the corporate structure, the work–life balance renews the challenge leaders as well as employees who work virtually have in being a productive unit. My research and studies continue to expose the positives and negatives associated with this new work structure. We continue to see employees distracted using technology such as smartphones, tablets, and instant messaging as a way to try and communicate and stay connected to the work environment. Leaders communicate through e-mail messages, instant messages, often foregoing face-to-face interactions as the speed of work increases. The world is getting smaller due to technology being infused into the work environment and the expectations of reaching employees anytime in any place are in full swing.

This fable highlights the trouble a leader can encounter by relying on technology alone as a way to lead a department. It is my belief that technology is a tool to help lead and should not be the sole means to conduct business. Vic struggles with the idea that he is making life easier by using technology as a way to lead his department. His expectation is that by using technology he is making the human perceptions of trust, isolation, and presence clearer to his department but finds out he is not getting the results he wants.

I strongly believe that the human perceptions of trust, isolation, and presence play a critical role in managing all aspects of building a team, especially a virtual team. It is even more important to have these human perceptions as a barometer as to the health of the individuals who make up the team (department) and the overall health of the organization. An organization that has a high level of trust, it has individuals who do not feel isolated and having individuals feel a strong sense of presence within their environment will make it the most productive it can be. Leadership is a critical part of setting the right message for the department. Managing the three human perceptions discussed in this book will establish a foundation that will not crumble under pressure.

Please join Vic on his journey of leading his team and glean from him the lessons he learns from his informal board of directors, Reliable Reggie (trust), Solitary Samantha (isolation), and Being Bob (presence). Together they must be managed effectively to strike a balance needed to lead a productive department.

Acknowledgments

It has been said that writing a book is a journey. As with any journey it normally cannot be done alone for it to be successful. This book is a case in point. I would not have been able to complete this book without the support of many people.

My wife, Rhonda, has not only been inspirational to me in making Virtual Vic come alive, she has inspired me to keep going when I questioned the concepts in this book. She provided guidance and often confirmed that it was important to get the story of Vic out to the world in a time when leadership and the challenges of the virtual work environment are starting to manifest within many organizations. Rhonda, thank you, for your unending support and guidance.

Andrew and Brittany, my children, have also provided support. Often their support could be misunderstood when they would tell me, "Dad, enough about Vic; just finish the book." I know they understood the concepts discussed. Now that they are productive adults making their own mark in the world, it is with much appreciation they have stood beside me on this journey. They even helped "Pops" learn newer aspects of technology; thanks, Andrew and Brittany.

My son-in-law, Adam, has also provided support and guidance. As a marine officer who was serving our nation in Japan during the time I was writing this book, he (and my daughter) with the use of technology provided the ability to keep a family connected while being many miles apart; talk about remoteness.

To my mom and dad, who have both passed away, I can never thank them enough for all the support and encouragement they provided. Without their care and lessons throughout my life this journey would have been difficult to endure. My mom passed away during the final edits of the book and I ask that you read the personal touch section to understand the great lesson she taught me related to the use of technology.

To my dear friend Lou, who was not only my father-in-law, but a friend who helped me shape many of my thoughts about Vic before he passed away. The talks we would have when we spent time together were life lessons that will never be forgotten. To Margaret, my mother-in-law, thank you for helping me define who Vic is and introduce his informal board of directors by discussing with me Reggie, Samantha, and Bob.

To all the virtual workers and leaders who have dedicated themselves to this new organizational structure, thank you. Without you my studies and research would be without merit. It is because of you that we must find better ways to lead and work within the virtual work environment.

All the teachers and professors who helped shape my thinking along the way, I say a big thank you. I am sure some of my high school teachers are wondering what happened to me to turn me into a writer and researcher. They need to know that providing guidance and staying on me to complete my studies while encouraging me to use my energy in a productive way has yielded results. The professors who worked with me during my undergraduate work and into my PhD, I cannot thank you enough. Dr. Salmon and Dr. Forsythe, in particular, thank you.

During my professional career I have had the honor to work for some of the best leaders. Under the leadership of Tony Cataliotti, Ellen Glover, and now Tom Ferrando, I have had the opportunity to learn from some of the best and been able to grow as a leader .

My coworkers and colleagues, I want to thank you for your support throughout the years.

I have had the privilege to lead some of the finest individuals in my leadership roles. It is my true belief that I was able to lead and grow as a leader because we worked as a team. There are too many to name, but they know who they are and I want to thank them for their support throughout the years.

The illustrations of Virtual Vic and the other characters where done by a very talented illustrator, Melanie Judd. Melanie was able to take my concepts of the individuals and bring them to life. Thank you for your dedication and hard work.

A special thanks to my lifelong friends, Kevin, Cathy, and Sarah as well as Sarah's husband, Corey. Kevin, Cathy, and Sarah have been my friends since elementary school. We have recently reconnected and have not lost one ounce of connection. I thank you for a lifetime of memories and with the inclusion of Corey we have found new memories that have inspired me to keep going. Our renewed friendship has been extremely important to me in knowing regardless of the distance at times, a true connection will endure any challenge.

Finally, as with all successful journeys there is a sense of accomplishment; yet, without readers this journey may fall short. In advance I thank all the people who will read the story of Virtual Vic and gain some connection to it. I hope that you are inspired by the story and can take some practical lessons as you continue to work in this new organizational structure. Like all successful journeys, journeys that are accomplished provide inspiration for us to do more. I plan to make other journeys related to the virtual work environment, and until that time, thank you all and I look forward to seeing you on future journeys.

Introduction

This management fable is about a person whom I call Vic, Virtual Vic. His story might not be exactly like yours or one you have experienced or witnessed. It will very likely be similar to a part of someone else's story, say a close friend, neighbor, family member, or maybe even yours. If not all, at least parts of his story related to technology involved in the virtual work environment (VWE), and how he deals with the challenges will ring a bell. We are experiencing a time in organizational structures when the trade-off between technology and the human interaction to leading others in the workforce is being stretched and stimulated beyond what management theories contemplated. Technology is challenging the human aspects of trust, isolation, and presence outside what humanistic management ever thought.

The purpose of this book is not only to introduce you to Vic but also to get you to start thinking about actions, in this story Vic's actions, as they relate to his management and leadership style and approach. This management fable relates to his role in managing and leading his staff in the VWE. He is leading a blended workforce, some colocated and some virtual employees. The book is also intended to make you think of his dependency on technology and how he uses it in situations he encounters within the VWE. Vic takes us on a journey through the human perceptions of trust, isolation, and presence related to his new job in a new city and the struggles he experiences leading his staff in the VWE.

This management fable of Vic is not about how his attempts to use technology highlights that the VWE is a bad thing, but rather it is about finding a balance when working within the VWE. Simply relying on the technology while ignoring the human touch creates leadership gaps for Vic. This book is meant to make you think about better ways to manage, perform, and lead in the VWE. Ultimately, the purpose of this book is to illustrate lessons that can create a more productive VWE. We all must deal with this new work environment, as it is part of our organizational structure for the foreseeable future.

Vic learns his valuable management lessons about the VWE through the use of three characters. The three characters become his informal board of directors and mentors. These characters represent three human perceptions that are extremely important in working and managing within the VWE. The human perceptions of trust, isolation, and presence create the foundational human perceptions. Reliable Reggie focuses on trust; Solitary Samantha focuses on isolation; and Being Bob's focus is about presence. Vic develops a way to measure these three human perceptions (he calls it the TIP scale) on a regular and ongoing basis. His TIP scale is a way to measure the human perceptions and get a sense of the stability the individual and the organization have while working in a VWE.

Vic meets Reliable Reggie, who is an ex-military officer. Reggie led troops in wartime and has dealt with life and death decisions. He was successful because he was able to establish trust within his troops and he led them with clear and direct communications, thus creating a deep trust among his troops. He was able to gain the trust of his troops by always being open and transparent with them. He worked extremely hard to make sure that he was committed to his troops at all times and in all situations. He never broke his promises and created a reliance not only on himself but amongst the troops as they related to each other. Reggie now works in community programs that support and help youth who struggle with trust issues. He is devoted to his beliefs and can often be found working out and staying in shape, so he not only can talk to the youth he works with but also participate in events that require a youthful body and mind. Reggie understands that trust is a very special human experience.[1] He understands that we cannot trust rules or technology; rely on them yes but trust no.[2] He is a stout 55-year-old man who appears much younger than his age. He continues to keep the military look and approach in his daily activities.

Solitary Samantha is a woman who unfortunately lives on the streets. She was once a very productive employee and was on her way up the corporate ladder until she was eventually laid off because of a corporate merger. The merger resulted in her working in a remote office as a virtual

---

[1]S. Sinek. 2013. *Leaders Eat Last* (London, UK: Penguin Books), p. 74.
[2]Sinek, *Leaders*, p. 74.

employee until she became disconnected to the new corporate structure. She was unable to find another job as she had lost her self-confidence after being laid off. She stayed in the town she once worked in and now lives on the streets. She became very isolated while working as a virtual employee and now remains isolated while living on the streets. Samantha misses the days when information about her job was communicated to her by management in face-to-face meetings. She understands the effectiveness of belonging and being part of a cohesive team. She learned being part of a larger, dispersed team challenged by distance erodes the concept of humanistic management, causing a loss of human meanings. Unfortunately, she lost her job while learning this lesson and now longs to reenter the workforce as a productive worker.

She spends her days walking around the city and spends her nights around local hotels looking for meals and shelter. She is a lonely person, feels extremely isolated, and is very cautious when trying to establish human relationships after being let go from her job. She would like to reenter the workforce but finds it very hard to even interview for jobs as she feels out of place since she lost touch with the corporate environment. She hopes each day that she will be able to reenter corporate America.

Being Bob is a small-business owner who has worked for a family-owned business all his life. He took over the family business when his father had an unexpected heart attack and passed away. He was thrown into a leadership role after his father passed away and had to find a way to keep his family business going. He has seen his family business change over the years; with increased population the influence of larger box stores entered his area created a new environment. Bob has had to make very tough decisions about his business over the years and has found a way to survive in a very competitive environment. His very small local grocery store has grown to be a mid-size store, but he has remained true to his family roots of running a customer-focused grocery store. He has successfully used technology to keep up with the best practices in operating a retail business, yet combines the older, more traditional aspects of customer service with the infusion of technology. Bob is African American and is recognized within the community for his outreach to other small and minority-owned businesses. Bob remembers and lives by a passage he read in a book written by Simon Sinek called *Leaders Eat Last,* where

Sinek discussed how money was developed to help expedite and simplify transactions by eliminating bartering.[3] Bob likens this to technology, which helps expedite and simplify communication and the relationships we build. However, just as money can't buy love, technology can't buy true, deep human relationships.

Bob has been able to provide his employees and customers with a store that provides a customer service model that nicely blends the old and new and offers both full- and self-service options. He has used technology not as a crutch to lower his cost but as a tool to provide the best service to all, while establishing human relationships that make his business unique. His staff connected with patrons and they in turn supported his business.

Given that backdrop, let's see what the management fable of Virtual Vic is all about.

---

[3]Sinek, *Leaders*, p. 18.

CHAPTER 1

Virtual Vic

I am extremely excited as I have been offered an executive-level position in a new city. I am entering the prime of my career. After all, I have worked for almost 20 years in corporate America, and I have witnessed its technological transformation. I am now ready to use the latest technology as a way to lead my department in becoming a very productive team. I find myself anxious yet excited about taking on the new responsibilities with my new job. The business world is evolving, and I am in a position to influence how my new company will operate.

I know I am ready for this new job that I have accepted. I am even excited about the new company and the new city I will be relocating to with my family. I am going to be an executive in corporate America!

On to the new job

After kissing my wife and kids goodbye, I headed to the airport to catch a flight to my new destination. After working through security at the airport, I showed my preapproved Transportation Security Administration (TSA) pass to a person who points me to a line. There was a guard standing there who is somewhat overseeing the process, but he simply points to a barcode reader. I placed my electronic boarding pass, which I had preloaded on my phone, onto the reader. I walked through the terminal and arrived at Gate A6; this is where I will board the plane that will take me to my new adventure. My plane was ready for boarding, and I walked into the plane after again properly scanning my barcoded ticket from my phone under a different reader.

After the mandatory prerecorded announcements, I settled in my seat and started to ponder how my first day would be. Will I set the right impression? Will my staff be responsive to me, and will they accept my way of doing business? These are some of the thoughts that ran through my mind. I have read many management books and felt prepared to lead my staff. I plan to use technology to communicate more effectively with my staff and handle the workload. I am confident that using technology will make me more available to my staff and them to me. The use of technology will also allow me to be more productive and efficient. The assignment of tasks, activities to benefit the department and enhance employee growth will be easy to share and we will be able to increase the number of actions and be more effective because of the reliance on technology. I will also ensure that I don't isolate those who work remotely, and we together will develop a strong and operative work presence. I jot these thoughts down on my iPad, which is connected to my Dropbox. Since I have access to the plane's Wi-Fi, I can already be more efficient in starting my new job not to mention as a frequent flyer I get the use of Wi-Fi on the plane for free.

After a safe and uneventful flight and landing, I was off to the hotel. But first I had to get my car. This was easy because I could go to the right space where my car was parked as the space number was highlighted on the car rental board that had my name on it. The car already had the keys in the ignition and all the paperwork was completed. As a frequent traveler I got the benefit of a car rental membership. This made things easier, and I was able to even book the rental with the app that was loaded on my smartphone. I never needed to talk to anyone about renting a car. All I needed to do was to drive out of the lot. I thought, as a new executive this is how it should be. In actuality, it is that way for anyone who travels and joins a rental car membership. Car rental organizations have everything prearranged, so you can function as a self-reliant traveler if you are a member.

While I was on the plane I used the hotel app to check myself in. So, when I got to the hotel, I parked in the self-park area for my convenience. Since I had already prechecked into the hotel, the self-park area was the easy choice for me. I walked into the lobby and right up to the precheck-in area where my room key was in a file waiting for me.

After getting my key it dawned on me how I was able to get on the plane, pick up my car, and check into the hotel without needing to interface with anyone. Wow! Technology really had its benefits.

I was tired from the trip and all the excitement, so I figured I better go right to bed when I got to my room. After unpacking I set my wake-up call using the self-service system on the phone in my room. I also noticed a new devise I had heard about in the hotel room. It was a sound machine that could be set to several different settings. These settings would allow you to drift away while thinking you were at a beach, play the waves button; at a camp site, play the water stream button; or at any place you wanted to be while actually in the hotel room via a button for white noise that would block out the world around you and let you be present where ever you wanted to be while actually in the hotel room.

I reflected again on the ease and efficiency that technology has brought to travelers and consumers. In the days before computers and automation, everything seemed to take much longer. I used to have to talk and explain to people what my needs were and get their help in getting me to where I needed to be. With technology I was able to do all of this without anyone else and it seemed so easy. Somehow as easy as it was I had a strange feeling of doubt or loneliness and wondered if I were doing things right. Did I really need someone to help or just be there? The human touch was mine and mine alone.

My mind was racing with thoughts of being so self-reliant, yet, at the same time, worrying with thoughts of whether I did the things I needed to do, properly; after all I did these without the help of others. I thought about a book that I had read a few months ago called *Loneliness: Human Nature and the Need for Social Connection* written by John T. Cacioppo and William Patrick, where they discussed the invisible forces that link one human being to another. They argued, "Our brains and bodies are designed to function in aggregates, not in isolation."[1] Here I was functioning in isolation and doing things all by myself, yet I felt conflicted, alone empty and wondered if I had someone helping or guiding me, would I be doing things more efficiently? Even though I felt good about doing things that I needed to do to get me where I needed to be, I still had a feeling of loneliness.

After a little unpacking and planning for my first day I laid down on the bed and fell asleep I woke up and felt refreshed. After a shower and getting dressed, I went downstairs to the lobby and was greeted by the front desk attendant, who asked if I needed any help, I politely said, "No," but the attendant insisted on helping. All I really needed was my car that had been valet parked upon my arrival. I asked for directions because I was worried that just using GPS might not tell me about the local traffic issues. The attendant who got my car gave me detailed instructions about how to get around town and what areas to avoid. I thought to myself without all these details I might have been lost in back allies and stuck in traffic as the GPS might not highlight areas to stay away from. The attendant stopped traffic to let me out of the busy hotel driveway and made sure that I was headed in the right direction.

After a short ride later, I arrived at my new work location. I walked into the main lobby where there was a sign greeting me as a new employee. There were also two company sponsors, one from my department and the other from the human resources department. They were there to help me get acquainted with not only my new surroundings but also the people I would be working with. The sponsors had arranged to have a coffee round table meeting for me and my department. They took me around and introduced me to other people in the building. They told me they arranged a lunch for me; they would provide presentations about

---

[1] J. T. Cacioppo and W. Patrick. 2008. *Loneliness: Human Nature and the Need for Social Connection* (New York, NY: W.W. Norton & Company), p. 126

the company and arranged a question and answer period, so I could ask questions as needed. They even prepared a list of restaurants I could go to for dinner after my first day. Once I decided which restaurant I wanted to try, they would arrange all the details for me. This included making sure I was greeted at the door by the owner of the restaurant to see if there was anything special I wanted. Talk about a human touch.

The meetings went off without any issues and the people were great. I was very excited about working at this company that seemed to have a culture of collaboration and a focus on people over process. The day ended, and I looked forward to the next day, when I would start my one-on-one meetings with my staff and we would start to set goals for the company.

After a great meal, I went back to the hotel, valet parked my car, and headed into the hotel lobby. I was greeted by an attendant who asked if I needed anything and welcomed me to the area as she knew it was my first day at my new job. I went to my room and received a reminder note about making sure I called my family and to set a wake-up call. There was a knock on my room door and when I answered, I was handed two hot chocolate chip cookies. Again, I was asked if I needed anything and was wished a good night.

I called home and started to tell my wife all the details of the day. I told her about all the people that catered after me and all the help they were providing when I suddenly woke up and realized I was having a dream, actually a nightmare. I had been startled awake by the ringing of the phone. I noticed my heart racing and I was in a cold sweat. I reached for the phone and heard the recording of a woman's voice say, "This is your wake-up call; enjoy your day."

I thought to myself, as I cleared my head, thank goodness that was just a dream, so my wife didn't have to actually hear any of that. She would have so many questions about me interfacing with all of these people and how they wanted to make me feel part of my new surroundings. This was not what I had expected. I had planned to rely on technology to navigate through my first day and didn't think it was going to be necessary to interface and rely on others.

My wife and I had talked before I left, and we anticipated that with all the technology available I wouldn't need to interface with too many people, if any at all, since I was so prepared to take care of myself. I didn't want to bother people and appear like I was not self-sufficient. After all, we discussed that in the age of technology and me coming into the company as an executive, I didn't want to appear needy. We discussed how I would need time to establish trust with the new people and in doing so I wanted to be careful I wasn't interfering with their regular routine. Even though I would not be relying on other people, she wanted to make sure I didn't feel isolated with not interfacing with people. Since we had gone through all the plans the weeks leading up to my arrival and since I was self-sufficient, I would have a level of presence that would not interfere with anyone else's time. I would create a level of presence without taking time away from anyone. Shaking off the cobwebs from the dream, I refocused on the real plan and the start of the day. I was now ready to get things going.

After a shower and getting dressed, I was off to the office. I went down the stairs and right out the side door to the self-serve parking spot where I had parked my car the night before. Once inside the car, I pulled the directions out of my briefcase, those that I had printed from the computer days before and showed the direct route to the office. I confirmed these with my GPS which was on my smart phone. Neither identified the local traffic problems that I found myself in moments later. I was now in major rush hour traffic jams. Oh, how I wished I had known about the local traffic problems. Not to worry, I thought. I can find a different route later once I am in front of the computer and I can put in different parameters on the GPS direction app to search for alternative directions. After a long delay from what I thought would be my travel time to work, I arrived and parked in the back lot of my new building.

Upon arriving at the office, I walked to the back door that had a card reader and swiped my badge, which had been sent to me a few days earlier. I went up the back stairs and into my new office. It was a large office in the corner of the floor, which had plenty of windows and overlooked the back parking lot.

I hung my jacket up and sat at the nice wooden desk that appeared all set up for my arrival. I saw a note (on the keyboard of my new computer with the large flat screen) that read, If you have trouble logging in, please call the help desk at 1-800 helpdesk. I tried unsuccessfully to log in, so I picked up the phone and called the number listed on the note. I heard a recording that said, "Press 1, if you are a new employee." I was then confronted with a list of other options. After listening to them, I chose Number 3, which was for log in problems. When I was connected to that line, I was faced again with a series of options. After listening to those, I pressed 3 again and hoped that would get me to where I needed to be. More options and another 3 was my choice. After this choice, it seemed like I would be getting the help I needed; however, as I listened, it seemed as though none of the options fitted my situation, so I pressed 9 to repeat the options. After listening a second time and determining that none of the options worked for me, I pressed 0, as instructed, to get a service person. After some music and an advertisement about how good the help desk service was, I heard a voice that said, "Sorry, no one is here right now to help; please call back," and the phone went dead.

I was not too discouraged by the events as I had my own iPad available and was able to get on the Internet from there. Once on the system, I was able to get to the online help desk. I sent a note requesting help. I received a note back asking if I was employee 8675309j4r. I responded that I was indeed that employee, and they sent me directions on my iPad that allowed me to log into my new computer. I was now off and running.

My first thought was to see each of my employees, but that was quickly overcome by the idea that instead of having to figure out which one I would see first, it would be better to send an e-mail to all my employees; that way I would reach them all and no one could say they were the last one I talked to. I wanted to treat everyone equally. Yes, treating each of them the same was the way to go. I was concerned that my virtual employees could also feel like I was treating them differently since I couldn't just walk into their office and talk to them.

I drafted the note; it was short and straight to the point.

Hi, I am in the office; I look forward to working with each of you. I would like you to send me a list of your activities and tasks as well as a presentation of areas you think you can improve on. Let me know if you need anything. I look forward to a very productive time with you and want you to know I am here for you should you need anything.

I hit the send button and then quickly went looking through the e-mail that had piled up in my inbox. I thought how different it was that even before I started I was getting e-mails, not like the old days. Many of the notes were system generated about the policies and procedures for using the computer, and they explained how to manage the load of e-mails and storage capacity. I even had a note about the instant messaging system the company used and how this was recommended as the best way to have internal discussions. I noticed that I had received an immediate response from one of my employees, saying how much they looked forward to the change with my leadership and how they saw this to be a great time for the company.

This person went on to say because they were approved to work from home their work–life balance was so much better, and they thought they were so much more productive. They mentioned how they hoped I wasn't going to change telecommuting even though the numbers for the group weren't as good as they had been when they all worked in the office together. This staff member mentioned that the complaints from the clients who stated that they never see the program manager anymore were already being addressed and I don't need to worry about those at this time. I wondered why this person thinks it is OK not to be seen and the complaints about the lack of presence was something that they could deal with without help or changing their way.

I went back to the e-mails and then started to go through the reports that showed the company's financial situation. I noticed that several other welcome e-mails started to come in from the other staff members but didn't stop reviewing the reports to read each of them.

After having my head down in the reports, I finally noticed, by way of my stomach growling, that it was lunch time. I thought how odd that with all the e-mails no one had stopped by my office. I thought about the conversation with my wife about feeling isolated but quickly laughed that off. I reflected on how I had communicated to my staff with the e-mail and thought about how so many people now preferred to send an e-mail rather than do a call or have a face-to-face discussion. I remembered reading a passage by Sherry Turkle in her book *Alone Together*, where she discussed how the new technologies allow us to "dial down" human contact.[2] I laughed at myself for thinking I was feeling isolated. After all I had communicated to my employees and many of them had communicated back to me.

---

[2]S. Turkle. 2011. *Alone Together* (New York, NY: Basic Books), p. 15.

I wanted to finish the reports and start work on my first 90-day plan. I remembered seeing a vending machine in the hallway close to the door I came through several hours ago. I ducked out of the office and headed for the machine. When I got to the machine I realized I only had a few dollars with me. I had forgotten to get more money before I rushed off to the airport the day before. I got some crackers and a soda and went back to my office.

I jumped right back into the reports and studied them for a few more hours before I realized that I had not responded to the e-mails from my employees. I went through a list in my head of the employees who had responded and found that one person had not responded all day. As I was still learning about each of my employees, I pulled up my list, which included their titles. As I worked through the list, I started to draw some opinions about the employees on the basis of their responses and the time it took them to respond to my initial note. When I reached the end of the list and matched each of the employees, I determined that the one employee who hadn't responded all day might be my problem child so to speak. I matched the name and the title against those I had received notes from and concluded that my director of human resources (HR) was the only employee who had not responded. I thought to himself, not a good first impression this person is making; after all they are in charge of HR and can't even find the time to respond to my e-mail. I wonder what they are working on that is so important.

After closing up the files and logging off from my computer, I headed for the door. Still no personal visits, and that seemed strange. I did recall seeing people pass my office. I had even saw one of my employees who sent me an e-mail moments after they passed my office, they sent an email rather than stopping in to talk. As I passed the vending machines going to the back stairs to leave, I remembered that I needed to get money. I could do this on the way back to the hotel by stopping by an ATM machine as my bank was a national bank that had ATMs almost everywhere.

As I passed a busy section of town, I spotted an ATM with a drive-up lane right next to it on the corner, so I quickly pulled over and proceeded to the ATM lane. I reached out of the window and punched in my PIN to withdraw cash. As I waited for the request to process, I looked at the almost empty gas tank and was reminded that my car was not full when

I picked it up. I thought, don't people do their jobs anymore? How hard is it to just make sure there is a full tank of gas in the car? I bet it was one of those automatic returns without the prepaid gas and they just returned the car low on gas. Come on, don't people care anymore? With the window down and the transaction almost complete, I smelled a wonderful aroma. I was also monitoring my e-mails on my iPad and noticed a few coming in from the virtual employees, but none from that (HR) employee who worked at the office. I thought these virtual employees seemed to be working longer hours.

After getting the cash and pulling out into traffic, I couldn't get the aroma out of my head. After all, the lunch of crackers and soda didn't really do the trick. I knew I needed to review a few more things back at the hotel so a sit-down dinner was not in the plans. I started to think about the home-cooked meals I had when I was growing up and the delicious meals my wife always made. I decided that is what I wanted—somehow, some way I wanted a home-cooked meal. As I proceeded toward the hotel, I saw a billboard that showed a lovely pot roast and vegetables with a caption that read, "The taste of a home-cooked meal without all the hassle."

I noticed that it was a grocery store advertisement and started my search for the store. I came upon a gas station a few blocks later and pulled into the self-serve pump. I got out, put my credit card in the gas pump card reader, and filled my car; while waiting for the car to fill up, I happened to look across the street and noticed the grocery store that had been advertised on the billboard. The pump stopped; I returned the nozzle, took my receipt, and returned to the car. I was pleased the grocery store wasn't out of my way, as I really wanted that home-cooked meal. I pulled across the street to the store, walked in, and noticed a very large section with a salad bar, hot soups, and a variety of cooked meals with the logo like the one I saw on the billboard. I made my selection: hot roast turkey with mashed potatoes and all the trimmings. I even added a salad from the self-serve salad bar and off I went to check out.

I was observing how large the store was and made a note to myself that I thought this would be a good store for my wife and kids to get to know. As I approached the checkout lines I noticed a handful of self-checkout stations that didn't seem crowed, so I proceeded toward them. I read the directions, placed my items on the scanner, put my credit card in the slot, and was all checked out. Off I went to my car with my freshly made salad and my home-cooked meal, well almost home-cooked meal.

I arrived at the hotel with the bag still hot and rushed through the back door that would lead me right to the hallway where my room was. I set up the office desk not only to do work but for my meal as well. I took a can of soda out of the in-room bar that was set up to make it easier for the traveler; I knew that the soda would be recorded on my bill and began to read my papers while having my meal.

As I read, I reflected back on my first day while also thinking how the meal was good but not how Mom or my wife would have made it. I continued thinking about the job and just couldn't move past the one individual who didn't respond all day. I made a note on my iPad to make sure that I pulled this individual's past performance reviews. I wanted to see if my hunch that this employee might be trouble was true. I hoped that their performance was documented, or was it a typical situation that people would just let things slide and look past things rather than confront the issue? I shut down my computer and put my papers away. I finished up dinner and besides the potential personnel issue that I might have to deal with, I concluded that my first day was a very successful one and looked forward to tomorrow.

I decided to get ahead of this situation with the director of HR so I sent a text message right then. I would show them that there is no time like the present to address an important issue. The text message was straight to the point. Message from 759-555-5478: "Not heard from u today; was wondering if there was a problem? Please get report as called out in my 1st note 8/14/18 by 10 a.m. with any Qs. I look forward to reading it and getting back to u with thoughts." I sent it with no signature line as I was sure all my employees had my cell number and the director would know who this important note was from. I had included my cell number as part of my signature line when I sent my first note.

I was getting sleepy and wanted to finish the successful day off with a movie that I could get right there in the room; like the soda it would be added to my room bill automatically. A Pay Per View movie would surely end the day on the right note. I decided I would see an old classic, *It's a MAD MAD MAD MAD World*, would do the trick, so I ordered that up to start at the beginning of the next hour, which was just 10 minutes away. I could settle in and make a call to my family before the movie started.

I reached for the phone and remembered I needed a wake-up call, so I programmed that in like the day before, remembering the dream (nightmare) I had the night before and took a deep breath, thinking how different my real day was in comparison. I called my wife's cell number, as that was the best way to reach the family, but there was no answer. Must be in a bad cell spot, I thought, as I listened to the recording: "Hi, if we don't answer we must be busy, running from one place to another; your message is important so please leave one and we will call you back."

> Honey, it's me. I am getting ready to settle in for the night and watch a movie before I go to bed. Sorry I missed you. Today went really well; I think I am going to do fine here—the office is nice, and the people seem to really respond to me. The city is nice, there are a lot of neat things to do, and I even had a home-cooked meal; yeah, not as good as yours but it was home cooked. I think you are really going to love this place. I can't wait for you to see it and I know we will be OK here. There seems like a lot of nice people around. I love you and miss you, Vic.

During the movie I was reminded about how crazy things can get and how the movie started with a major traffic jam very similar to my drive to the office. I fell asleep after the movie.

In this story, we see how Vic made some choices that had a different result than what he had planned and expected. He used technology that might have actually hurt his ability to gain trust with his new employees. He may also have created a judgment about one of his staff that could be totally wrong. By using technology and making himself nonpresent to his staff, he might have isolated them or at the very least isolated himself. Ultimately, what he tried to do was give his staff space to do the right things but that might have created a level of lack of presence that could create a divide between him, the place he works, and the employees he is to lead.

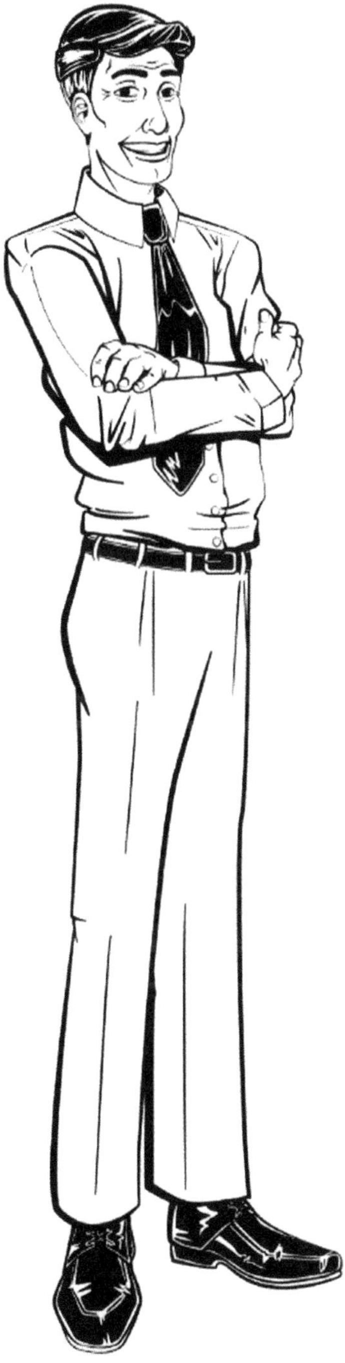

CHAPTER 2
Vic Meets Reliable Reggie

Several days had passed and e-mail after e-mail, I was having difficulty getting a positive response or at least the one I was expecting from my staff.

I would get responses but they seemed to lack the overall energy and commitment I expected I would see from the people who reported directly to me. After all, I was making myself available to them and finding ways at all hours to reach out to them and make sure they knew I was available around the clock to help them with any issue that might be getting in the way of their work.

Trust was a huge goal for me. I wanted to make sure I established trusting relationships with my staff and I was wondering if I had already failed in doing that. It was a strange feeling for me even after a very short time I was already experiencing the human perception of trust. Was that the reason I was not getting the expected responses? I knew in today's business world trust was needed more than ever. The landscape of business was ever changing and with the introduction of the VWE (virtual work environment) trust would be paramount. I told myself, and I knew that business was conducted through relationships, trust was the foundation to establishing those relationships; without this the work could not get done and the business was fail. I also knew that without trust people would just go through the motions and not really feel the commitment to working with each other and making their work environment a productive environment.

I thought about the first weekend I was on the job and that I knew one of my staff was struggling with a report. This employee had sent me several e-mails telling me they couldn't get the report to me as they were struggling with the aspects I needed in the report. I called the individual on the weekend and was able to catch them on the phone early on Saturday morning. I spent about two hours working with this individual going over the aspects of the report and shared my ideas by drafting up a few reports and sending them to the individual while we talked. I figured this was a big help to the individual but when we met on Monday no more progress was made on the reports. When I questioned the individual why no more progress was made, the individual explained that they had personal plans for the weekend and wasn't able to give any more time than the two hours on that Saturday morning.

I was puzzled because on the phone call the individual seemed to be engaged and committed to getting the report done so we could discuss it on Monday. I thought how this was an odd response since I had made myself available. I just couldn't understand why the commitment wasn't mutual. I counseled the individual that these reports needed to be completed and I had relied on the fact that they would get them done. I was frustrated by this lack of reciprocal commitment.

I thought to myself this was getting to be common problem when it came to the reliability of my staff. I thought I am making myself available, so why is it so difficult for my staff to do the same? I felt that this broken commitment was a big trust issue for me now related to this employee. As they left my office I had a feeling like I couldn't trust them.

I started to conclude that the aspect of reliability comes from the concept of the ability to be trusted. I thought I was expressing trust to my staff but often felt my staff didn't trust me.

During my stay at the hotel, I came to meet Reliable Reggie, as I called him. I assumed he was another guest at the hotel where I was staying while I settled into my new location. This individual seemed very confident in the way he carried himself. He was a somewhat older gentleman but had the appearance of youth by his actions and mannerisms. He appeared to be either still in the military or to have recently left the military. I often saw this individual at the hotel gym. When I would come back from work I would see Reggie at the hotel gym working out on a regular basis. I began to view this person as the one constant in my day. I wondered to myself how this individual could always be in the gym. How could he be so committed and show such dedication to his workouts?

After one particularly hard day at work for me I came through the hotel lobby and passed the hotel gym. Once again, I saw him working out and having an overall persona as he normally did. He was dedicated and interfaced with the other people working out. He seemed to have an approach to life that regardless of what the day brought in terms of challenges, he was in the gym working out. On this day I decided that I had seen enough and was determined to go meet this individual. I went to my room, changed into my workout clothes, and decided I was going down to the gym and see if I could have a conversation with him. I wanted to meet him since he appeared to be so reliable and had a sense of trustworthiness.

I went to the gym, and as predicted, he was still there. The gym was a smaller room but large enough for multiple people to get a workout. I started to do some stretching and noticed that he was doing his workout like I had observed many times before. I observed him talking with others in the gym and overheard him introduce himself to another guest of the hotel working out. He introduced himself as Reggie. After a few awkward minutes I approached Reggie and said, "Hi." Reggie stopped his workout and acknowledged the introduction.

Reggie took the time to engage with me and I asked how he was doing. I politely said that I was fine but was having one of those days. Reggie acknowledged and told me that he had observed me being at the hotel lately and that he often saw me rushing through the hotel like I had a lot on my mind. He commented that even though he had seen me in the gym before I lacked the real commitment of working out and it appeared I was going through the motions of working out but not really getting the benefit of working out.

After that comment, I thought, do I really share with this stranger all the trouble I was carrying around the trust issue I was having with my employees in my new job or just simply let it pass? After all, there was something intriguing about Reggie that made me want to meet him. So, instead of just saying everything was fine, I decided to take the chance and share with him my feelings related to the trust issue. He seemed very trustworthy, and I thought what is there to lose. Trust is about exposing yourself to others. Talk about trusting someone I didn't even know with my personal feelings. Trust is not only about the reliability to do what is expected of the person you give trust to, but also about the ability to do what is asked of them. So, I took a big chance with Reggie and made myself vulnerable and thought he could be reliable in what I was about to ask of him. I also had to believe he had the ability to handle what I was going to confide in him. We have all met people who by the way they carry themselves and handle their environment indicate that they can be trusted. The opposite is true where we have met someone and by the way they carry themselves or communicate they don't establish a level of trust right from the beginning. I had to take the opportunity to find out what made Reggie always seem so committed and reliable in terms of his workouts. I wondered if he was so dedicated to his workouts as he dedicated this to all aspects of his life. What drives a person to be dedicated and committed?

I told Reggie I had recently moved to the area to start a new job.

Reggie asked me whether this was a good thing or a bad thing.

I responded by saying it was a good thing but that my expectations were not matching up to what reality was providing.

Reggie asked why this was the case.

I said that I had come to take this new job as a senior executive but was struggling getting my staff to respond in a positive way. I felt there was level of trust that was not being established. It almost seemed the harder I tried the less trust was established. I wasn't getting a reaction out of my staff by asking them to respond to me by way of my e-mails and off-hour texts.

Reggie told me that trust was one of the fundamental aspects that all relationships need to have in order to be productive. After all, without trust there is little chance for a strong relationship to form. This is where I was confused. I was giving my staff space and freedom to do what they needed without trying to control their actions or call meetings to discuss things I wanted to emphasize the departments focus and forward direction.

I knew that business was conducted through relationships and trust is a big part of relationships. My staff would need a positive relationship not only with me but with each other. It appeared the staff had trust toward each other but it was not developing with me. When trust was part of the workplace and present at all levels, people would be excited about what they do. It was clear that my department was not excited about what we were doing, and therefore, trust must be missing. The connection that trust would create was missing.

We both laughed but there was a surreal aspect about that comment that made me want to ask more about it.

So, after taking a deep breath, I asked Reggie if he could expound on his comment about trust being a foundational aspect that relationships needed to be productive.

Reggie told me that without trust it is very hard to establish a relationship that can be relied upon and that the relationship would be only superficial without a deep level of trust. He said that recent studies showed that the level of trust between employees and managers was on the decline. He told me to only look around at some of the major events that had occurred in the business world. He mentioned the Enron scandal, the Sarbanes–Oxley Act, and how banks had lost so much trust from people with the banking crisis that occurred. These were major events that directly addressed how trust was lost. He mentioned these large public dealings as examples but then said it is not just these big events that erode trust but many smaller actions have the same effect on trust as well.

Still intrigued by where this conversation was going, I pressed the conversation.

"Reggie, can you tell me more?"

Reggie said that maybe the best way to explain this concept was to tell me a little about his background.

Reggie was a retired military officer and had led many troops into some very hard missions. He told me that during his military training the aspect of trust was second to none. He explained that there was no time to question the level of trust that had to be established between the members of his unit when they were performing life and death maneuvers. He explained that trust wasn't something that could happen at the time it was needed but had to be established long before the real need for it.

I was now fully involved in the conversation and asked Reggie if he could tell me what he thought was happening to me and my staff.

I wanted to see if Reggie could offer some ideas to help me with my trust issue.

Reggie said that he would be happy to help if he could but cautioned me that there was no one-size-fits-all approach for the establishment of trust. He went on to say that trust was a human perception that had to be shared by both individuals involved in the relationship. Just because one person has a high level of trust doesn't mean the other individual will share the same level of trust. Trust was something that had many facets to it. It could take a long time to earn it but only seconds to lose it. He told me that just because I wanted it doesn't mean that I was going to get it. Trust is a very personal human perception. He mentioned that it had to be worked on by the people trying to have a relationship and emphasized that just because one person was doing things that they thought was trustworthy others might not see it that way.

After a few more minutes Reggie suggested that I take the rest of the evening and try and define what trust meant to me and how I portrayed trust to my staff. If I were willing to do this, we should meet at the gym again and talk about that first.

I agreed and we finished our respective workouts and bid each other a good night. I left the gym noting to myself that I was encouraged about the action Reggie had given me and I looked forward to our next meeting.

I went to my room and began thinking about the questions Reggie had asked me.

At first, I started to look for a definition of trust. I concluded that trust was mutual and that both individuals who wanted a trusting relationship had to give to each other to establish trust. I went on to define the aspect of trust by saying that there had to be a commitment associated with each individual. If one person didn't live up to their side of the commitment, trust would be damaged. I also started to think about how I started to feel a lack of trust toward my staff because they were not living up to their commitments. I recalled the first day when I sent out an e-mail to my staff and how some individuals didn't respond right away to my e-mail. I laughed to myself about how that one individual had not responded all day to my e-mail and I thought, what could this individual be working on that was so important that they couldn't respond? You will recall this was the HR director.

I thought more on the definition and what I was doing to establish trust with my staff. I concluded again that I was living up to my commitment and thought about how I had called one individual on that Saturday morning about the reports and was disappointed on Monday when the reports weren't done.

I finished thinking about my definition and was ready to talk to Reggie the next day. I concluded that the definition I would share with Reggie was going to be, trust had to be a shared perception and there had to be a reliance on and vulnerability toward each other. It has to do with a confident belief in the other person or an entity. It implies a reliability, dependability, and capability.

I went to work the next day and was excited for the day to be over so I could go talk to Reggie about the definition I had developed related to trust. When the day was over I rushed to the hotel and quickly changed and went to the gym to find that Reggie was not at the gym. How can this be? Reggie was always there. We had talked about following up on the conversation and I felt the level of disappointment I had experienced with my staff. I did my workout but it lacked the excitement and commitment that I had hoped the new definition of trust was going to give me. This time my workout was even less productive because I was focused on dealing with the disappointment of Reggie not being there as planned. My feelings really seemed to be related to the feeling I was having with Reggie not being, the disappointment was a big deal. How could he break the commitment we had talked about the day before?

The next day was the same in terms of work and I started to lose interest in talking to Reggie. I was still intrigued by the concept of trust and the definition Reggie had asked me to come up with, yet I started to feel more disengaged with Reggie. It was a strange feeling since I had met Reggie only 2 days earlier, yet the disappointment in the missed meeting left me feeling somewhat empty. I thought how this was a feeling I had when others had not lived up to their commitments. I reflected on my definition and found that many of the aspects I thought defined the aspect of trust were challenged when Reggie didn't show up.

I arrived at the hotel the next day and walked through the lobby and saw that Reggie was again in the gym. I quickly changed and went to the gym. When I entered the gym I immediately walked up to Reggie and confronted him about not being there yesterday. I said that I was at the gym yesterday and was there ready to discuss the definition but was disappointed that Reggie did not show up as planned.

After a long pause Reggie asked me if I had set a time for them to finish their talk or if I had made an assumption that Reggie would be available when I was ready. This took me aback and made me think about our conversation. Reggie was right. I never asked Reggie if he would be at the gym the next day; rather, I just assumed that Reggie would be available. I had made this assumption on the fact that I had always seen him at the gym and since we had talked about talking again he would be there.

Reggie said that this was the first lesson in establishing trust. Do not assume that the other person understands the unspoken commitment. One individual cannot assume the commitment is clear and understood by all. He went on to say that just because you are ready and available doesn't mean that everyone else is. When trust is truly established there is no doubt as to the expectations and the outcome.

I thought how simple that was but how easily that was taken for granted. I apologized for making the assumption that Reggie would be available. Wow, I thought, making assumptions really can set things off course. Even when there is an assumption, which might be wrong, the feelings associated with trust are compromised. Trust turns to distrust in a matter of seconds when the perceived commitment is broken.

Lesson two was now clear. Communicate well-defined expectations and established goals that are understood by all. Reggie told me that if I would have asked his availability I would have known that Reggie was not going to be at the gym the day before. He told me that he had other commitments that would not allow him to be at the gym. If I had asked him about meeting again this would have been clearly understood that the next day was not going to work. I briefly thought that he could have told me but realized what was important to me, meeting the next day, which was my priority, was not his. I owned this aspect and it was not right to simply think since it was a critical issue and the meeting was important to me he shared the same sense of urgency. It was very reasonable for him to think we would talk the next time we saw each other and even though my time frame was the next day his time frame was different.

This encounter made me begin to think that maybe the way I was showing trust to my staff was not appropriate. After all, I thought, since I was the manager all my staff should be ready to do what I had asked. However, just because I thought I was holding up my end of the commitment didn't mean my staff were sure about what they were supposed to do. It dawned on me that even though I was trying to be trustworthy, trust wasn't really being established as much as I thought. Maybe I wasn't clear and my staff hadn't understood my expectations.

I decided I needed more time to be able to have a more productive conversation with Reggie and I would need to spend more time thinking about the definition of trust and get back to Reggie with a modified definition. Based upon this I asked Reggie if I could take the night to think about it more and talk to him the next day. I made it clear to Reggie that I wanted to meet him at the gym the next day at 6 p.m. to continue the conversation and before Reggie could answer I quickly asked if he would be available. With a slight smile on his face Reggie said that he would be available and looked forward to talking again.

I left and thought how I felt better about being clear and reflected on the level of trust I now felt toward Reggie and compared it with the day before when my trust was waning. I thought if I could establish this feeling with my staff, things would start to match my expectations.

I concluded that my original definition of trust was not wrong, as there was no real true definition of trust because it had to have a personal interpretation. Rather, the definition needed to include the concept I had read in a book called *The Trust Edge* written by David Horsager, who wrote about trust in this way: "Trust is more like a forest—a long time growing, but easily burned down."[1] This was like the comment Reggie had made about trust taking time to be established but it could be lost very quickly. This concept was odd because even though I had not grown a long-term relationship with Reggie, in one moment, I was willing to burn it down when the meeting was missed. If trust was this fragile in long-term relationships, look how fast it was disrupted in short-term relationships. My relationships with my staff were all but a few days old; had I already disrupted them by my actions?

---

[1] D. Horsager. 2009. *The Trust Edge*. (New York, NY: Free Press), p. 10.

I thought and thought about how trust was indeed a two-way street and I needed to do a better job in laying out clear expectations and defining goals associated with the commitments and I needed to really work on establishing trust with my staff. After a few more thoughts I concluded that trust was defined by me as the expectations of the behaviors of others, and the perceived motives and intentions in situations entailing risk of the relationship of others. There was a clear reliance on each other to develop trust in all relationships and more importantly to me I needed to work harder to establish these clear lines of communications since some of my staff were remote while others where physically present. This mix of staff could cause confusion among my staff. I wanted to be careful that my actions would not burn the feeling of trust for any of my staff. Would the staff who were physically located with me have a different interpretation associated with the expectations than those who worked remotely?

I went to work the next day and noted to myself that those who were remote often questioned me more than those who were colocated with me. I reflected on the fact that I often spoke to them in the exact same way and now realized that might have an adverse effect on some of my staff. Why were there so many more questions being asked by those who were remote? I concluded that it must be that they lack the level of trust because they are missing something in my communication. The more I thought about it, it became clear that those who were not present lacked the other aspects of my communication. They lacked the body language and the nonverbal signs when I spoke to them. They only had my voice or my written words. They did not benefit from the nonverbal cues not only from me but from others who were present and they could react to the others who were present.

I went to the gym that night and was anxious to tell Reggie how I had modified the definition of trust. I explained my new view of trust and shared the story about the forest with Reggie. Reggie smiled and confirmed I was now seeing how fragile and important the aspect of trust was. Reggie told me about his experience in the military when there was no doubt that trust was shared by all. He said that without the reliance on each other's behavior could result in a loss of life for him or others during his experience in the military. He jokingly said that there was no room for burning down the forest in the time of war.

Reggie asked me what I had learned by working on the definition of trust.

I responded by saying I had learned that I could not assume any aspect of my communication. I had to be very clear and make sure that the goals and expectations were shared and understood by all. Reggie nodded with approval and then said that the third lesson of trust was now ready to be told.

The third lesson about trust is that it has to be worked on all the time. He went on to say that once trust is established it must be maintained and that it required consistent diligence to ensure that trust remains strong. I cannot forget this and must always look for ways to check the level of trust among my staff. I cannot let the ugly stepbrother of trust creep into the workplace and that ugly stepbrother is distrust. Broken promises, poor communication, and ignoring the signs of confusion will result in distrust, which will ruin all of the hard work in establishing trust.

I was committed to working on this aspect with my staff. Reggie reminded me that there was no one right answer and that the human perception of trust was different for each person. It was different because everyone had different life experiences and as a leader I was responsible for learning those aspects that could relate to each individual in terms of establishing trust.

I said I understood and thanked Reggie for his time and the lessons he had given me.

I left the gym that evening more committed to establishing trust with my staff and realized I was in large part in control of how much trust could be created by my actions.

I thought long and hard about the way I had treated my staff in terms of laying out expectations and how I might not have effectively communicated to my staff. I thought again about how I had concluded that those who had not responded to me related to my first e-mail because I was not clear in expressing that I wanted a response. I thought I could have done that differently and saved a lot of frustration on my part as well as theirs.

I went to work the next several days with a desire to be clear in my communication to my staff. I took time to make sure that my expectations were defined and sought to get agreement from those I was working with. I also started to interface with my staff with face-to-face interactions and called those who were remote rather than sending out e-mails. I found the face-to-face interactions were much richer in a sense of communicating and I was able to read the body language as I spoke to the staff located with me. I started to use Skype meetings with my remote staff and found that even though it wasn't exactly like being in the room together, seeing their faces through the use of technology was yielding better results.

A few weeks had passed when I ran into Reggie again.

Reggie asked how things were going and I responded by saying that the level of trust I was feeling was on the rise and that there was less confusion with my staff in terms of expectations. I told Reggie that my staff seemed to open up to me more and they shared with me in their discussions their level of vulnerability was apparent and that made the relationship feel more trustworthy. Reggie nodded with approval and told me I appeared to be well on my way to gaining one of the cornerstones of leadership—creating a high level of trust.

Not everything was perfect but things appeared to be headed in the right direction. I still wondered why all my staff were not responding as well to this new level of trust.

I soon realized I was struggling with different types of staff. Those who were remote were still slower in establishing trust than those who were colocated with me. I noticed that those who relied more heavily on electronic versus face-to-face communication had more trouble with trust.

Maybe there were other things I could be working on like I did with trust. Even though I was working hard on my communication skills and my commitments there still might be some differences with the remote staff compared with the colocated staff.

I promised myself I would continue to work on effective communication daily with all of my staff and I would look for other aspects that might be making the difference. It was then that I realized it might not just be the aspect of trust that was a challenge with the remote staff but it might be that they are perceiving a sense of distance.

I would take some time to reflect on this and hoped that I could find a solution to this sense of distance as I did with the aspect of trust.

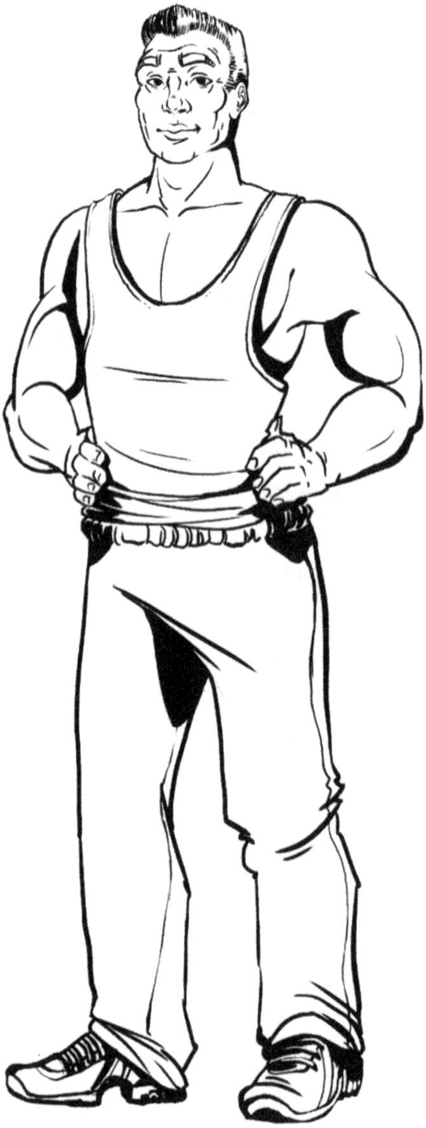

CHAPTER 3
Vic Meets Solitary Samantha

After my encounter with Reliable Reggie I knew there was still work to be done to reach the optimum performance and productivity from my staff. I was proud of the newfound appreciation for trust and how I would use that in my leadership style going forward. Reggie had really made me see the positive and negative side of trust in a way that I had not fully realized before. If trust was so fragile, how can so many people just take it for granted, like I did with my staff? I thought about how there were still certain people I felt I was not reaching in terms of clear communication and direct expectations, thus not fully reaching a level of trust I thought was needed.

I continued to evaluate my staff and the multiple ways my staff was situated in their work environment. Some were local and in my immediate presence while others were remote and didn't have the benefit of being in my presence and me in theirs. Was this working situation something I would need to address or was there a way that I could reach all my staff whether colocated or not? I knew that the new work environment, the VWE, was becoming more and more popular. I knew my staff was made up of workers who were colocated with me; some workers who were completely virtual, working miles away from the office; and still others who had flexible work schedules and were considered part-time virtual workers.

I started to look at each of the groups and concluded that each posed different challenges for me in terms of leading them. After the lessons I learned from Reggie I thought I needed to develop a better approach of connecting with all my staff but would need to customize the approach with each of the different types of workers.

I started to think about how my staff reacted in different ways and wondered if it were because of where they worked. It made me think deeply about what motivated people to work and where that motivation came from. I thought about a passage I had read years ago about the concept of self-efficacy. Self-efficacy is certainly worth having as Henry Ford famously put it, "whether you believe you can or you can't, you are right". Gandhi perfectly understood the pivotal role that self-belief plays in our lives:

> Your beliefs become your thoughts. Your thoughts become your words. Your words become your actions. Your actions become your habits. Your habits become your values. Your values become your destiny.

I was most bothered by the group that was completely virtual followed by the part-time virtual workers and then the colocated staff. There appeared to be a different level of connection of each group not only with me but with each other. I knew to get the most productivity out of the department I needed to find a way to get these groups to work as a cohesive group regardless of where they physically worked. Gandhi's words really took hold now. What were the beliefs of these virtual workers and did they differ from those of the colocated employees? If their beliefs were different, was that translating to the issue that was bothering me in terms of their connection to me and the department because their values ended up being different?

As I thought more about this it took me back to how I had observed Reggie at the gym and recalled also seeing a lady who always was around the hotel. This individual never came inside and appeared to be homeless. This lady was often seen trying to talk to some of the hotel staff. She would interface with them in the back and by the exits where some of them took their breaks outside the hotel.

The lady dressed in clothes that were soiled and often had a look of despair on her face. She also appeared very lonely and disconnected with the environment around her. She would drift into the background if more people would gather around her and seemed to limit her interactions with people.

I committed that I would observe her the next few days and thought maybe I could approach her to find out what she was about.

One day as I arrived at the hotel parking lot it was raining so I hurried from my car to the back door of the hotel. I noticed this lady standing by the back door, trying to stay dry from the rain. It was an awkward moment as I had a key to open the door and knew that she did not.

As I opened the door I asked if she would be willing to talk to me and invited her inside the hotel, trying to help her get out of the rain.

She acknowledged me and took me up on the invitation to talk. I believe she really used my invitation to get out of the rain.

I commented that I had seen her around the hotel and asked her if she were staying at the hotel, even though I had concluded she was not a guest. As we walked from the back door toward the lobby, I thought we could talk there. Others passed us and gave us an odd look. It was obvious to others that we made an odd couple. She appeared to almost hide behind me as others passed and was shy in making eye contact or acknowledging the other people.

When we reached the lobby, there was an area somewhat away from the main area where tables were set up for people to gather. I asked if this was an OK place for us to sit, and she said that was fine.

Once we were seated I asked her what her name was and she said it was Samantha. She never made eye contact with me and appeared very isolated, almost like she was in a different space even though we were there together. I recalled this feeling and look when I used to be uncomfortable in my surroundings. The feeling I was comparing this to was when I was in situations that I really didn't want to be in. Another example of how this made me feel was how people often find comfort with animate objects to give them a sense of security of not feeling so isolated or afraid. I remembered the movie *Castaway*, with Tom Hanks playing a character who was on an island all by himself and he found a level of comfort with a volleyball he named Wilson, or when at times a parent with a very shy child will put sunglasses on them to make them believe others couldn't see them as long as the glasses were on. This look of connection or projection on or by something else rather than what was real made them find a level of well-being.

I introduced myself with more details about myself, trying to make her more comfortable. She was intent on listening to me but lacked the overall connection I had expected in a one-on-one conversation.

After telling her about my new role and why I was staying at the hotel I asked her why she was always hanging around the hotel. Samantha looked up at me and said I would not understand and tried to change the conversation back to me.

I told her more about my job and started to explain how I had different types of workers who made up my department. I explained that I had staff in three groups and that they all made up the department; yet, I was already feeling different about each of them. As I told her about the colocated staff she had little reaction to that, other than to say she understood what working in the traditional environment meant. I started to explain the other two groups, the part-time and full-time virtual employees when she interrupted me saying I know how tough it can be to work away from others. She seemed to show a level of connection and appeared to be somewhat emotional in her response as she proclaimed that she knew it was very difficult working apart from others.

I felt for a moment we had a breakthrough in our conversation and we might be on to something with this topic so I asked her how she knew about this.

She became quiet again and looked away. I was confused on why the virtual workers seemed to strike a reaction from her but then she stopped talking. I tried again to ask her how she knew about working virtually and she took a deep breath and then started to talk.

She told me that she at one point was a very productive employee for a company in the area. She mentioned how she was moving up the corporate ladder when the company she worked for was acquired by another company whose headquarters was located in a different town in a different state.

She explained that her performance was very good and she was a valued employee. She said that the new company liked her very much and wanted to retain her services. They told her they would be willing to allow her to work there since they had plans to keep a local office and that she could work remote from the main office. She wasn't sure how this was going to work out and she had concerns with being a virtual employee, having always worked in the traditional work environment. After all, she had never worked away from her peers and was worried that distance would be hard for her. She commented on how with the rise of technology she thought she could use Skype and instant messaging to keep the real-time communications going with her peers. She explained how she was encouraged to try this but had seen the loss of personal touch happening even among colocated employees, who often would send e-mails to each other rather than stop by each other's office to talk or ask questions. She recalled overhearing a couple of her coworkers talking about how their personal lives had changed with the use of smartphones. These workers spoke about how they would often use their smartphones to leave voicemail messages and send e-mails rather than talk face-to-face. They further commented how this use of technology allowed them to avoid real-time commitments and how it was a way to lessen the human touch. She even recalled a few hard conversations with others she had worked with and how the e-mails were cold and she knew if these conversations would have taken place face-to-face they wouldn't have been so distant and cold.

She talked about how after a few months other people in the local office started to get laid off and that there started to be a disconnection between the local office and the headquarters. After a few more months the new company decided to close the local office because there seemed to be a loss of productivity coming out of this office. They were still very pleased with her work and offered her to stay on and told her she could work from home. They wanted her to stay on but thought this was an opportunity to save money by closing the office.

Samantha paused the story to see if I was still paying attention. When she realized I was paying attention she asked me if I had ever visited my virtual employees. With a level of embarrassment, I told her no. I quickly told here that I communicated with them on a regular basis.

I told her that I sent e-mails to them, called them on a regular basis, and even used the company's instant messaging to communicate more frequently, thus making them feel as if they were in the office with the others.

Samantha smiled and said, "I see."

I thought this response was odd and asked her why she responded as she did.

Samantha told me that this is what most people think when they are the ones not working virtually or away from the other staff members. She went on to say, "Just because you think you are involving them through the use of technology, you are missing an important part of what it takes to make a team cohesive and connected."

I paused and said, "Do you mean I am not communicating to these people even though I am?"

She told me that it is not just the mere fact of communicating but how I was involving them in the decisions that were being made that affected them and the overall operations of the department.

I felt myself getting defensive about this: After all, who was she to tell me that my communication style was not a good one? I recalled the conversation about trust and communication I had with Reggie; this seemed to be taking a different path. After gathering myself, I told her that the VWE was all about saving time and money for all involved. I went on to say that for the company there were savings in terms of physical space for less offices and the infrastructure associated with having an office for every employee. I felt for a moment like I was repeating what her company had told her. There were cost savings to the employee in terms of commuting and great flexibility for the employee in terms of work–life balance.

She then told me what I had felt a moment earlier: I sounded like her old employer right before they decided that she was no longer a productive employee. They had decided that by being away from the main office was not working out as they had hoped and they let her go.

I was now feeling bad about my defensiveness so I apologized and asked her to explain more about what had happened.

Samantha said it was OK as it was a common theme that she had heard from many people along the way.

I asked if she could tell me more about her situation. She obliged and said that as time passed she felt more and more disconnected and isolated from the others in her department. She explained how her manager had changed from the original one and her new manager was not effective in including her in decisions and changes that were happening within the company. She felt more and more distant and struggled to keep up with the mission of the company. She started to work longer hours and tried to stay active with the tasks that she was assigned. She went on to say that she felt she was still very productive but her manager continued to tell her that her work was not what he had expected and she had to redo a lot of her work.

She became quiet again and started to pull back into a private place. I started to feel this roller-coaster ride of emotions with her. She was connected and then retracted, engaged again, and then retracted. She appeared lost at times with the overall conversation, and I wondered what was causing this level of mixed emotions she was experiencing. Why was she isolated and alone even when we were together?

It was getting late and I needed to get some work done. I asked if she would be willing to talk more tomorrow and remembered the Reggie conversation and made it clear that I would like to meet her at the hotel tomorrow at 6 p.m. to continue the conversation.

Samantha said, "Sure, what else do I have to do?"

I said ok let's meet tomorrow and continue the conversation.

We said goodbye, and I watched Samantha walk out of the hotel door and vanish into the dark night.

As I went to my room I wondered what had really happened to a productive worker that ended with her being let go. There had to be more to the story.

I could not get the story out of my mind and went to the office the next day thinking whether I was doing something wrong with my virtual workers. I decided to send a note to them asking if they felt I was communicating effectively with them. Each responded positively and this confirmed to me that there was something more to the Samantha situation than just her feeling isolated. I was sure that I was communicating effectively to my staff and was ready to tell Samantha the results of my informal survey.

I arrived at 5:45 p.m. and found Samantha by the back door, standing alone as I had observed many times before. As I approached her she seemed distant. I asked her if she were ready to continue the conversation and she said she was.

As we went into the lobby as we did the night before, we sat at the same location. I was eager to explain to her about the results of my inquiry with my employees and she listened as I explained what I had done. When I was finished she asked me what else I thought they could say. Again, this took me aback.

I asked her to explain. This time she said that I needed to not be defensive and that I need to look at the situation from the virtual workers' perspective and not mine. She said this was the first lesson I needed to understand and that was not to judge the reactions of others only by my own point of view.

I agreed that I would listen and not be defensive. She said that the virtual worker is in a tough situation and that often they run the risk of having to say what they think the manager wants to hear because they fear losing the opportunity to remain a virtual worker. They might suffer from a lack of trust and because they feel isolated they might not tell exactly how they are really feeling about the situation. Often when a virtual worker talks about feeling isolated or disconnected the manager responds by saying, "You wouldn't feel this way if you were here." This creates a no-win situation for the virtual worker.

The no-win situation is a very difficult aspect related to the VWE. On the one side, the virtual worker can talk about being disconnected and feeling isolated and on the other side where does the feeling of isolation actually come from. Isolation does lend itself to the actual concept of working remotely and being away from others in the VWE, thus creating a built-in sense of isolation.

I asked Samantha to explain this concept further and help me understand how this situation was created.

Samantha continued to tell me how isolation was indeed created by the concept of working virtually but that this could be mitigated if both people, manager and employee, understood that extra effort would be needed to make sure that there was not a distance created by the situation. She explained to me that working virtually carried a heavy emotional toll on the virtual employee. Giving up the conventional work environment would mean leaving behind the network of coworkers and managers who often provided emotional support. The responsibility would be on the virtual worker to find new coping mechanisms for such things as rejection, self-doubt, worry, and task completion[1].

This was directly in line with the article I had read about the social learning theory. Kendra Cherry discussed in the article how during the first half of the 20th century the behavioral school of psychology became a dominant force. The behaviorist proposed that learning was a result of the experience one had with their environment. This was related to the association with and reinforcement of the individual's environment[2]—a shared learning that might be absent for virtual workers.

At this point Samantha felt it would be good to talk more about what had happened to her to illustrate how this feeling of isolation is a shared responsibility.

She went back to how her career was derailed by the fact that she was not fully involved in the discussions that took place about the organization that affected her. She explained that there were new policies and procedures put in place but they were primarily put in place for those who were colocated. She explained how ad hoc meetings would take place and decisions were often made at these ad hoc meetings. She told me that often decisions were made and then implemented without being communicated to her until she performed outside of the new rule. She mentioned that the incongruences started to pile up and that she felt further and further outside the decisions and the process that was now the norm for department operational cadence.

She explained in one example how the process for dress at the office had changed from a business attire every day of the week to one that had a dress down Friday. Her manager decided that it was important for her to attend a face-to-face meeting and authorized her to come to the headquarters for a meeting. The manager explained to her that he would arrange this meeting on a Friday because it would be easier for her to arrange travel and doing the meeting on Friday would give her greater flexibility to attend the meeting. What that really meant was she could reduce travel cost by traveling back on a Saturday; thus, she would have

---

[1] Alice Bredin, *Virtual Office Survival Handbook* (New York, John Wiley & Sons, Inc., 1996) 182.
[2] Kendra Cherry, "How Social Learning Theory Works" (Verywell mind, 2017).

to give up one of her days off for the betterment of the company's bottom line. Her manager also told her that they could do a Friday dinner, which would be more convenient for those who worked locally since they could arrange better plans around their normal work week.

Samantha arranged her travel and spent the night before laying out her business clothes to attend the meeting. When she arrived at headquarters for the meeting she walked in dressed in what she thought was appropriate and quickly realized that she was overdressed and the rest of the staff was in jeans and more business causal. She immediately felt out of place and very uncomfortable compared with the rest of the staff. Her manager was even in a pair of jeans and had a polo golf shirt on.

As the meeting started she also felt distant from the others as they laughed and shared stories about what had happened the other day in the office and talked about events that took place locally and didn't involve her.

At the first break several of the staff approached Samantha and asked her why she had overdressed and made comments about how out of touch she was with the new way of doing business. After all, the last time she had been to the office everyone was dressed in business attire.

She said to me, "You get the point, right?" This led her to tell me that it was time to discuss lesson two. If department policies or procedures were changed, it was the responsibility of the manager to make sure that all staff, those local and virtual, were made aware of those changes—that the changes had to be effectively communicated to all and no assumptions could be made that everyone understood them. She told me how important it was for her manager to help her understand the details around the meeting and not take it for granted that those working virtual should just understand the changes. She paused and asked me how I would feel if that situation had happened to me.

This question really made me feel out of place. Even though this had not happened to me directly, I did in fact feel out of place. This brought a very awkward feeling to forefront for me. I, for a moment, felt isolated from the group that Samantha was referencing even without being there.

I started to think if I had implemented changes that were not effectively communicated.

I asked Samantha how she felt about the situation in her example. She responded by saying she felt very isolated and out of touch with the department. She went on to say this was the beginning of the end in terms of feeling connected to her department. She knew she had to take on the responsibility to stay abreast of new policies and procedures, but how was she to know what she didn't know?

I asked what she had done about the situation and she replied that she didn't do anything other than feel uncomfortable and was sure she would not make that mistake again. She knew that if she were ever asked to go to a meeting at headquarters, she would check the dress code beforehand. She told me of a concept that often happens in a group, team, or department situation and that was groupthink. She explained this is the practice of a group of people who make decisions as a group and it stifles the creativity and ideas of individuals. The group values it shared decision and process more than those of individuals because of the cohesiveness that happens in the group. Samantha explained that those who worked together often would reach a consensus, groupthink, and the virtual workers would be left out of that cohesive decision.

She told me that she became very self-conscience of her dress and how she fit in with the rest of department. She mentioned that this was when her anxiety in dealing with her fellow department members and her manager started. Even though she knew she had done nothing wrong, self-doubt started to creep into her decision-making process.

She explained to me that she was now worried that she didn't fit in and that she worried if she would ever be able to be a productive member of the department going forward. The feeling of being isolated was now a consistent thought for her.

Samantha seemed to be getting bothered and uncomfortable the more she talked, so I thought it would be a good time to stop the conversation. I noticed the uncomfortable feeling by watching her body language so I thought it would be good to see if she would be willing to meet me the next day and start the conversation where we left off. I asked Samantha if she wanted to talk again tomorrow.

When I asked her if she wanted to stop the conversation and meet again tomorrow, Samantha said no.

She said we should continue and work through the difficult discussion. She explained that not addressing issues when they arose was also a big problem for her and what she believed was a major contributor to the decrease in her effectiveness. Each time she was having a *tough* conversation with her manager he would say, "Let's end the conversation and catch up in our next face-to-face meeting." She knew this was his way of pushing off the conversation and since she was not colocated and had no plans to travel to see him, this was a very convenient way to stop the conversation. She asked me how I would interpret that and said it's hard to do that if we are colocated.

I now felt a little uncomfortable, but realized her point. Since we were face-to-face it was much harder to stop the conversation without being rude so I went ahead with the conversation. I figured I might as well ask her why she wanted to talk rather than take a break, especially since she was the one who appeared to be uncomfortable.

I stayed silent and waited for Samantha to start the conversation again. Samantha gave me with an inquisitive look and asked if I were OK.

I responded with a tongue-tied answer. I said, "Well, it seems odd that you want to continue when you appear to be the one who is bothered by the conversation; so, why would you want to continue?"

She said, "Well, it is time for lesson three to be discussed."

Samantha told me that hard conversations don't get better with time and that if her old company had the hard conversation with her sooner rather than later, things might have worked out differently. She told me that hard conversations benefit both parties more than ignoring them and pretending things are OK when they really are not.

I was confused by this lesson and asked her to explain.

She went on to tell me that everyone understands that this is a business and business decisions need to be made. She told me especially with virtual workers who already feel isolated and disconnected that not addressing change and things that need to be addressed, place the virtual worker in a more difficult situation.

She told me that as a virtual worker she was already feeling out of sight and out of mind. Her manager was not addressing the real issues he was having and was prolonging the reality of the situation, meaning that the manager's expectations and hers were getting more and more different and therefore disconnected. She said that as time passed she became more anxious and felt out of touch. Each time the manager asked her to redo work, she was confused why there was a disconnect. She was, in her mind, working longer hours and trying to do what she thought was right but with each task it became more obvious that things were heading down the wrong path.

Finally, when things were at their worst in her mind, she was told that she had serious performance issues and that the only alternative was for her to separate form the company. She was caught off guard by the sudden conclusion that she had to leave the company.

She told her manager that she was willing to do whatever needed to be done to fix the problem and that she thought she was doing what was asked.

Her manager told her that this was coming for a long time and that she should have seen this coming. Her manager went on to say that she should have realized that she was not performing up to the standard of the company and at this point they had to move in a different direction.

Samantha asked what could be done and the response she received was that she should find a job where she could be more connected and that she would be given two weeks to transfer all of her work to another employee. The manager said they were sorry that this occurred and that their expectation had been that she would be able to handle working remotely but concluded that it was not making sense any longer to try and make this situation work.

He told her that someone from the human resources department would be in touch with her in a day or two and she should start to get her tasks together so they could be transferred.

Samantha was lost: She had no idea what to do and she had not been looking for other employment and felt totally alone.

Samantha had a few days of vacation so she decided she needed some time to gather her thoughts and sent a note to her manager that she would be taking the next couple of days as personal leave before she could start the transition.

Her manager was somewhat harsh when he told her he would approve the vacation but expected her to do what was needed to make the transition successful.

Over the next few days Samantha became more and more despondent with the situation and found herself having very negative thoughts about the company and her future.

After a couple of days, she packed up her files and made arrangements to transfer them to the employee who was identified to take over her responsibilities. She shipped her files to the main office and called the person who had been identified. After several calls that went unanswered she finally reached the person. She was told that they would review the files, and if they had any questions, they would be back in touch with her.

Her final day came with no follow-up calls and she performed her last day feeling completely defeated and confused.

I was taken aback by the events that were just told me and could only ask the most awkward question left and that was, "How did you end up in the situation you are in now?"

Samantha, now with tears in her eyes, said that after facing this situation she lost all confidence in her ability to be a productive member in any organization. She tried to find another job but continued to shy away from taking on challenges since she had lost confidence and was afraid she would repeat the mistakes of the past. After several months of not working she found it difficult to reengage in the business world and things continued to spiral downward for her. Without a job she had to move from her apartment and was not able to find another one because she was unemployed. After staying with friends for a few weeks she decided that the only choice she had was to try to make it on her own. This resulted in her living on the streets. She became more and more discouraged about her ability to join the workforce.

The anxiety and feeling of being alone took on greater importance for her and she started to live on the streets as that was the only way she could deal with her new life.

At this point I said I was sorry and she responded by saying, "I don't need you to feel sorry for me; I need you and the rest of corporate America not to place workers in such a horrible situation again." She went on to say that she once believed that the VWE was a good thing and even with all the bad things that had happened to her she still believed that it was a good thing as long as everyone involved in it understood how simple things taken for granted were addressed.

I followed up by saying, "Like what?"

She reminded me of the three lessons she had taught me and said, "Don't lose sight of the human being who makes up the VWE and always address the issue rather than ignore it." She told me that once a person is taken out of the traditional work environment it is hard for them to reenter and that it is extremely important not to lose sight of the fact that they need to be included; otherwise, the feeling of isolation will creep in and once a person feels disconnected it is hard to get them to feel part of any organization again.

At this point I didn't really know what to say, so I said that I had learned several very valuable lessons and would be committed to never let my virtual employees feel disconnected.

She thanked me for listening and told me that this was the first time in a long time that someone had really taken the time to identify with the human touch that she had lost so many months ago.

We concluded our conversation and I thanked her again and we said goodbye. As I did a few nights earlier, I watched as Samantha walked out of the lobby and disappear into the dark of the evening.

I thought about the valuable lessons I had learned about how human beings can be and are affected by their work environment and how people, whether colocated or not, had to be cared for. Even though business decisions needed to be made, they needed to be made with a humanistic approach to ensure a company's most valuable asset; the workers are cared for regardless of the business decision.

As I went to my room that evening, I thought about how trust and now isolation were two very important human perceptions that needed the focus of all leaders. I wondered if there was yet another human perception that existed that strained the human aspect of working in a VWE.

VIC MEETS SOLITARY SAMANTHA   45

CHAPTER 4

Vic Meets Being Bob

I have now encountered two individuals who taught me a lot in a very short amount of time. I will cherish the time I spent with both individuals. I will always refer to Reggie as Reliable Reggie and will call Samantha, Solitary Samantha. They will forever signify trust and isolation to me. I recalled the stories that Reggie told me as well as the lessons about trust. I reflected on the story of Samantha, who made me look at isolation in a totally different way.

I found the contrast between the two people I had met interesting—the confidence Reggie displayed in all his actions and the way Samantha seemed to lack confidence. The only time Samantha seemed to have confidence was when she spoke about her productive time with her company. Even though both taught me lessons about different aspects and different human perceptions, there appeared to be an overlap between them.

I would need to continue to think about this overlap and see if I could draw some sort of correlation.

I had already started to put the lessons from Reggie and Samantha into practice and had enjoyed their benefits. I had seen a more productive department, and the morale of the group seemed to be on the rise. There was still one aspect that I was struggling with and that was the concept of virtual workers. They seemed to have a different mind-set. It wasn't just a mind-set, they appeared to have a different level of presence related to their work environment compared with the other staff members. I realized I needed to manage them differently than I once thought. I needed to find why their presence was different; their concept of being engaged with the department troubled me.

This took me back to a scholarly book on presence I had read. There was a particular section that addressed seeing from within the organization. The authors addressed the *whole* organization and the difficulty of seeing the culture of an organization. Edgar Schein, a respected scholar dealing with organizational culture, said, "If you want to understand an organization's culture go to a meeting."[1] He discussed the aspects of who speaks at meetings, what topics are discussed or ignored, and the innuendos that occur. This made me think how important presence was to the culture that is developed. I wondered what he would say about my meetings. And more importantly what would he say about the virtual workers—how were they involved in the meetings? How could they see the body language or pick up on the innuendos?

I realized that the VWE is a newer way of running the business. I recognized that this new work environment gave me a chance to get the best people for the department regardless of their physical location. I liked the flexibility this working situation afforded my staff and saw the benefits of work–life balance.

Despite this, I still experienced some difficulties with the virtual workers and noticed that they lack a level of integration with the rest of the staff. The technology the company made available allows for this working arrangement but it appears it is used differently by many of my staff.

---

[1]E. Schein. 1992. *Organizational Culture and Leadership*, 2nd ed (San Francisco, CA: Jossey-Bass).

I wished that all of my staff felt present in the work environment and that they feel like they had all the tools available to them as the colocated employees.

Yes, here it is, the concept of self-efficacy: People do what they are most comfortable with. People will do what they believe is their greatest strength in their own ability to complete tasks and reach goals. Could there be a difference in what the colocated workers felt they could do and what the virtual workers believed they could do? Even if the tools and equipment were the same, did the difference in location (i.e., presence) affect the person's ability to believe what they could do to be productive?

I thought about the concept of presence and the issues that emerge for all of us in how and when we are really present. Presence is a human perception like trust and isolation. I began to acknowledge that for a person to have a strong level of presence they must feel like they are truly present in their surroundings. I thought about my staff who were working remotely and wondered if they felt present in their work location or if they were actually more connected to the physical location rather than the department. Can they really feel all of the aspects that the colocated staff feels? After all, if a person is not seen, can they really be present?

I reflected on my feelings about how I felt when I first arrived and no one really recognized my presence in the office that first day. I thought maybe I did this to myself by being so self-reliant and not looking for ways to make myself available to my staff. But then again, I was present, wasn't I?

As I sat at my desk I thought about how lonely I was feeling on that first day and the days that followed by staying to myself. I became aware of how important really being in the moment and integrating myself in the environment would make me feel a different level of presence. Having a level of presence should not be that difficult. If you are committed to the task and you are living in the moment, you should be able to express the level of presence to those around you. But why was this not working? Why did I feel physically present, yet a lack of being present?

This made me think about home and how I always felt present in my home with my family. I was very comfortable with my family and we all functioned with a level of connectedness. We could anticipate each other's moves and emotions. We knew how to read the body language and we knew what to say to help the situation we were facing. We were present with each other.

I thought about times lately when I really felt a strong level of presence not just by being physically located somewhere but having a deep awareness of the environment and connections to the surroundings. After I started making myself communicate more clearly as Reggie had told me, I felt more connected; translate that to more present. I tried to find times and locations where I felt this level of being present. The more I was engaged in my surroundings the better I felt about being engaged. As silly as it seemed, I felt more present in the hotel once I had stayed there a few days.

This took me back to going to high school. When I first went to class I didn't feel connected to the classroom or my fellow students, but as the days and weeks passed, I felt more connected to the class. I even laughed when I thought back to how I would always sit in the same seat as did the other students until one day the teacher rearranged the seats. We all walked in and stood there trying to figure out what to do. As we sat in the new arrangement I felt, as I am sure the other students did, like we were no longer as connected to the class as we were the day before. This simple aspect of not sitting in the same seat made me feel disconnected, and therefore, less present in my own classroom. Talk about being a creature of habits, thus a creature of feeling engaged in my surroundings.

My mind wondered and I thought about what I was going to do for dinner and how I had become a frequent shopper at the grocery store that I went to on my first day on my new job in my new city.

I thought a lot about how I always was able to find what I needed there and how the home-cooked meals always made me feel comfortable. I thought about the time I wanted to find a particular product at this store that was sold at my old store in my old town and the next time I went to the store it was there. How did this store always make me feel comfortable, and even more importantly, how did I always feel so connected to my trips there? It was like I was really engaged in the store and the store was engaged in me; there was a sense of being present.

Then it dawned on me. It wasn't the store itself or any of the physical attributes. It wasn't the convenience of the store or how the store was laid out. It wasn't the layout of the isles or as a matter of fact it wasn't anything physical about the store. It wasn't the advertising that was all over the city or even the discounts and membership club that the store offered.

It was the one guy who always seemed to be there. It was the way everyone who worked there was connected to the shoppers and the store itself. They all seemed to have a sense of pride and were really present, all the time. With every need that I had this guy was there. This guy was committed to making sure I received service and the level of attention that a customer should get. This guy was committed to being present for my needs and wants.

I thought, who is this guy who wears a name tag with three simple letters on it that spell Bob? I was now determined that I would go to the store tonight and see if I could talk to this individual. I wanted to talk to him like I had talked to Reggie and Samantha and see if he had lessons that would help me.

So I arrived at the store with a different mission in mind on this visit. I was not shopping for groceries; I was shopping for help with the concept of presence that I was experiencing.

I walked in and saw this individual and approached him.

The individual acknowledged me and asked if he could help me. I said yes but that the question I had was not about a product, but about him.

The individual seemed a little taken back but was welcoming to my inquiry.

I introduced myself, and the individual responded by saying that his name was Bob.

I asked if he had a few minutes to maybe help me with a feeling that I had every time I walked into the store. Bob said, "Go on." I told him that I always felt very welcomed and connected to the store. I commented that he always seemed to be attentive to the happenings around the store. I told Bob that there was a sense of integrating the shopper's needs and a focus on delivering what the shopper wanted.

Bob thanked me for the kind words and said he was still unsure as to what I needed.

I explained that I was new to the area and told him about my new role with my company and my staff. I told Bob that I had meet Reggie and Samantha and how they helped me deal with aspects that I had struggled with, which were trust and isolation. I was hoping that he could help me with presence in the workplace.

I told Bob that I was still struggling with the virtual staff and the feeling of them being present. I told him I had always felt present in the store and how the store provided a comfortable feeling for me. I wondered if there was something he was doing to make the shoppers feel like they belonged at his store.

Bob said that he would love to talk to me but maybe we should arrange a time to talk when he was not focused on overseeing the operations of the store. He suggested that we find a time when I could come back when there was another manager on duty and he would talk to me about how he operated the store. Bob told me that when he was the manager on duty he needed to be attentive to the happenings and he wanted to provide me with the attention I needed to understand the concept that he prided himself on.

Bob said that he lived by four elements associated with creating a work presence. He explained that these four elements were being focused, attentive, connected, and integrated.[2]

Bob told me that he would be available tomorrow anytime after 4 p.m., when he got off. I was feeling that I was taking time away from Bob, especially when he was off, so I asked if there was another time. I didn't want Bob to have to talk to me on his time off.

Bob responded by saying that when you really care about your work environment and when you have the job that requires you to care for others, you are never really off the clock.

We laughed as we both knew the demands of management. I told Bob that if it was alright, I would take him up on the offer and meet him at the store tomorrow at 4 p.m.

I shook Bobs hand and thanked him for the first lesson that he had not formally introduced but made clear anyway. The lesson on being focused was the first lesson associated with feeling present. If you are focused on the surroundings and you clearly understand your role, you are focused and you will feel present.

I grabbed myself an almost home-cooked meal on the way out and headed back to the hotel.

---

[2]A. Cuddy. *Presence: Bringing Your Boldest Self to Your Biggest Challenges* (New York, NY: Little, Brown and Company), p. 53.

The next day I really was focused on my role as a manager and found it easier to anticipate the needs of my staff as well as get the task at hand completed. This being focused really does translate to being present. I thought to myself, the more present you are, the more mindful you are of your environment.

I arrived at the store around 3:55 p.m. and waited for Bob to be ready for the conversation. Bob asked me to join him in the back office where we would continue our talk.

As I entered the room I couldn't help but notice all of the pictures of what appeared to be prior grocery stores. These pictures told a story all the way to a large picture of the store that I was currently in.

I asked Bob about the pictures. Bob began to explain but paused and said, "Let me tell you a little about myself first."

Bob told me that he comes from a background where he was around family-owned businesses all of his life. He took over the family grocery business early on in his life, probably before he was ready. He explained how his father's unexpected heart attack left him, the eldest son in a family of three, to run the business.

Bob's family business was very successful and had passed down through two generations, Bob being the third. When Bob took over the business it was still one of only two grocery stores in the small rural area where he had grown up. The area was just outside the major metropolitan area of a growing city, which now was my new home. It wasn't long before urban sprawl began and large developers began to buy up vacant land in Bob's smaller town, connecting it to the larger city.

Shortly after, big-box stores started to fill every corner from Bob's town to the larger city. With the increase in the number of large box stores came the introduction of quantity over quality in terms of customer offerings.

Regardless of how hard Bob tried to provide excellent customer service the customers seemed to be enticed by the convenience they saw in the larger, new grocery stores that came from areas far away that had been associated with the developers.

These new grocery stores presented efficiency and a self-service approach to the stores offering. This was designed to help the shopper move more quickly through the store and be self-reliant on getting in and getting out. These stores didn't need to hire more local workers; they just added more self-service checkout lines. They used technology such as barcode readers that the shopper could use as they put products in their cart and then just pay on the way out. They built large salad bars and bars that served premade meals for all occasions—breakfast, lunch, and dinner.

Bob's business started to suffer and he was not sure what to do. He recalled the look on many of his employees' faces as well as his customers'. They all seemed to wander around and go through the motions of either working or shopping. They lacked the connection they once had and lacked the feeling of presence.

Bob explained that presence isn't about the person who has the loudest voice, the biggest ego, the person who tries to control the environment. He asked me to think about the times I have walked into a group meeting and if I have ever felt a connection to someone, without even talking to them.

I responded that I have felt that.

He asked if I had ever walked into a group meeting and immediately felt a dislike for a person without even talking to that person.

Again, I answered that I had.

He said that is personal presence. The first person is authentic. They are real and they are engaged with their environment. They are not trying to control their environment; they are engaged with their environment.

Bob explained that having presence with others is about showing up first and foremost. This means literally showing up.[3] Once you show up you need to connect with others in a way that shows a level of connection with and influence over the people you have come into contact with.

Bob went on with his story and explained he knew he had to take action or otherwise he might have to close the family business.

Bob made a bold move and found a place closer to the city, which was now connected to the suburbs where he once operated the family business.

Bob opened the new store and brought many of his staff with him. As he closed the door to the old store and opened the doors of the new

---

[3] A. Cuddy. *Presence* (London, UK: Hachette), p. 70.

one, he was still bothered by the lack of the old feeling among his staff and shoppers—that of being connected to each other and the stores. He longed for the days when his staff interfaced with the shoppers and the shoppers enjoyed the time in the store and didn't appear to rush out after filling their baskets.

One day as Bob sat in the back office he found the pictures of the previous stores and had an idea. Why not go back in time and get the employees to feel what it was like in the older days? He took the pictures and had them framed. He then placed them in the back office, which all the employees visited on a regular basis, including when they took their breaks.

Shortly after the new pictures were placed on the walls he noticed his staff asking questions about the old locations and they remembered what it was like working in them. He also noticed with the questions being asked the employees started to work differently. They were more focused on their tasks and the shoppers. They were happier because they felt like they belonged there now and they took pride in wanting the store to have a feeling of a place the shoppers wanted to come to.

Bob knew that finding a way to connect the employees with the work environment was a very important part of making the employees feel present. This was lesson number two. To feel present, one has to feel a relationship with the environment. It is not enough to be physically present; one must have a connection that transcends the physical location and connects the individual with the environment, which is larger than the individual. This is about setting a culture and Bob found a way to do so by getting the employees to understand the history of the store and giving them a connection to the past that led them to the current environment.

This was a very important part of making his employees feel like they were present in the work environment and it improved customer services, which resulted in increased business.

I wasn't really sure how I might be able to implement this fully in my situation so I asked Bob if there was more to this concept of presence in the workplace.

Bob reminded me of the four aspects related to presence in the workplace. He asked me if I recalled those elements.

I said I did and answered by saying they were focused, attentive, connected, and integrated.

Bob was pleased that I had remembered them and told me that there was no one right answer in trying to develop a sense of work presence.

Bob went on to tell me about how he had to find a way to get his employees to be attentive to the shoppers.

Bob told me that his store was still facing fierce competition and that he had to get his staff to provide a level of service that exceeded the expectation of the shoppers.

He went on to tell me about the days when he was working for his grandfather and how regardless of what task his grandfather was working on he was aware of the overall status of the store. Whether he was in the back or helping someone load groceries into their car he knew what was happening in the overall surroundings of the store.

He said there was one particular day that he will never forget and that was when his grandfather was helping someone load their groceries into their car. Bob was standing outside getting the trash cans cleaned out and moving the carts around when his grandfather called him over and said, "Go into the store and help the individual who is looking for a particular brand of tomato sauce."

Bob went inside the store and to the isle where the tomato sauces were and didn't find anyone there. He walked around a little while and then went back out to talk to his grandfather about the individual he was sent in to help. He told his grandfather that he didn't find anyone. His grandfather finished loading the car and took Bob inside with him. He asked Bob to stay with him and they walked over to the produce section and found an individual with a lost look on their face.

As Bob and his grandfather approached the individual, Bob's grandfather reached down and grabbed a special tomato sauce that was advertised as *fresh* sauce that was placed on a ledge under the real tomatoes. He walked up to the individual and offered the jar saying, "Is this what you were looking for?" The individual said yes with a big smile on their face, thanked him, and went to the checkout counter.

Bob was amazed by the events that he had just witnessed and asked his grandfather how he knew what the individual was looking for.

His grandfather said that Bob had made a typical mistake, going to the obvious spot and assuming he would find the person who needed help only where the other tomato sauces where located. Bob's grandfather told him that he had to learn to be aware of his surroundings and not just look at the obvious spot. Awareness had to be all encompassing, covering the entire environment.

What Bob should have done was to be attentive to the situation and not look at the situation only from his point of view. Bob was confused and asked for more explanation.

His grandfather continued to explain that not all things are what they appear. Bob had to know that the store had tomato sauces in multiple locations and just checking one area was not being fully aware of the environment. If Bob had looked around and been attentive he would have seen the individual walking aimlessly around the produce section. He would have realized that not all tomato sauces were in the main isle and could have anticipated that there was another answer and not only the one that Bob thought was right. He explained to Bob that just because there is one physical location for some tomato sauces that was not the only place tomato sauces could be present in the store.

On the basis of that incident Bob learned to be aware and attentive; he had to look at the whole picture and not just look at things from his point of view. Bob now realized that just a common physical location might not lead him to the actual location where the service is needed. Bob explained to me that this is the third lesson. He had become attentive to all points of view in establishing the level of presence within the environment that created this situation in the store. I needed to now develop an awareness that encompassed my entire department not just the physical location I was actually present in.

Bob went on to say that if everybody only viewed the work through their point of view many things would be missed. Missing things leads to a disconnection and soon that disconnection can lead people to lose a sense of being present in the true environment. It was Bob's job to make sure that he created a level of presence by being attentive to the needs and desires of others. For Bob these were his shoppers; for me these were all of my staff, colocated or not.

I smiled and said that was an incredibly different way of looking at things. I knew what I needed to do, especially for my virtual workers: I needed to create a sense of presence from their point of view and not my own.

I asked Bob if there was anything else that had helped him create that particular type of culture.

Bob responded by saying, "If you remember the four elements of creating presence in the work environment and practice those on a regular basis, you should be able to create the type of unified culture I was trying to establish."

I thanked Bob and said I hoped to be able to talk to him again and wished him continued success.

Bob politely said I was welcome. While I was walking away, he commented, "If you stay in the moment and focus on the environment, you will always be present."

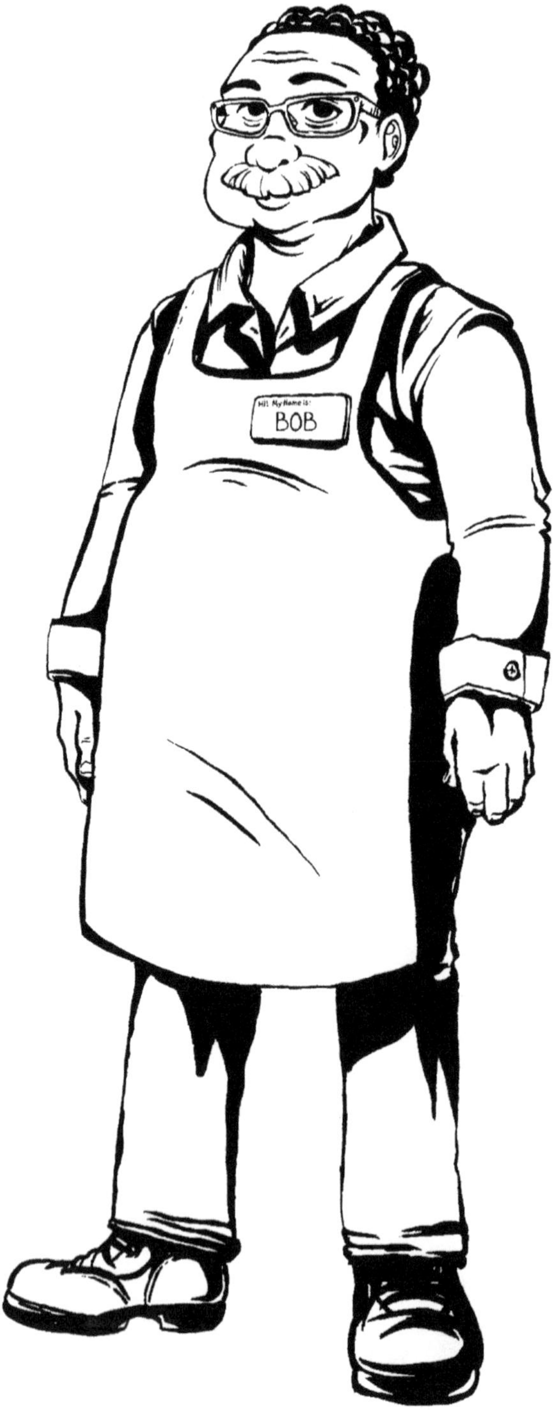
Hi! My Name is:
BOB

CHAPTER 5

The Department Meeting

I was now more motivated than ever to lead my staff. I was now armed with what I believed were the tools to lead my team to become a very productive department. I more fully understood the aspects of trust, isolation, and presence and how to deal with these human perceptions in a blended team.

The concepts I learned from my new, informal board of directors (BOD), Reggie, Samantha, and Bob would serve me well. The aspect of having a personal BOD is really important. Regardless of what role you have or the size of your company, having a personal BOD is critical for managing your success and the success of your department and company.

On the basis of the lessons I had learned and how I had tried to lead my team, I knew the first thing I would need to do was to call a department meeting and talk about the mistakes I had made during my first several weeks of being on the job. I would talk about the lessons I learned from my new, informal BOD, Reliable Reggie, Solitary Samantha, and Being Bob. The lessons I learned about trust, isolation, and presence needed to be explained to my staff so they too could take part in making the department the most productive.

I had to plan the meeting and I wanted to let my staff know that I was excited so I scheduled the meeting. I knew that I would need to get my virtual workers to attend the meeting. I remembered Samantha telling me about the meeting she attended on a Friday and how she was not informed of the latest policies.

I decided that I would not call the meeting on a Friday to make sure the virtual staff didn't feel like they had to take personal time for traveling back on Saturday. I also knew that I had to review any policies and procedures that had been updated lately and inform all the staff about them. I needed to be clear in my expectations and wanted to be fully engaged so my presence was felt. I remembered the concept of personal presence and wanted to ensure that all members would be engaged in the meeting.

After deciding that I would call the meeting to start on Tuesday afternoon the following week, I began to put the following agenda together:

- My first few days
  - My first attempt
  - My mistakes
- Lessons about trust
- Lessons about isolation
- Lessons about presence
- The TIP scale

I would have to structure the meeting as to not call out the staff for what they did but how I set the stage for the lack of trust, developing a level of isolation and creating a work presence that was about creating true engagement. It would be important to explain the concept of self-efficacy. As a point of fact, self-efficacy was part of a greater theory developed by Albert Bandura—the social learning theory, which addresses how observation, imitation, and modeling play a critical role in the way people react to their environment.

I decided that I would end the meeting with this new concept I had developed called the trust, isolation and presence (TIP) scale. This tool would help me manage the blended workforce by monitoring the levels of trust, isolation, and presence.

The TIP Scale

I figured out that the human perceptions of trust, isolation, and presence (TIP) needed to be in balance. If one of the human perceptions were interpreted as negative for an individual, that could result in a less than stable and productive outcome.

I figured out that someone who didn't trust at the right level would be more focused on looking for ways to distrust others. I knew that if the trust level were low, the relationship could not be optimized. I also knew that when the level of trust was low, it would be very hard to make the group productive.

I determined that if someone felt isolated, they would not be able to be productive related to the mission of the department. I remembered how Samantha lost her confidence when she became isolated and knew any individual with a loss of confidence would struggle in their tasks. Finally, when it came to isolation, if a person were isolated or felt isolated long enough, it would be hard for them to reintegrate themselves into the department.

When I thought about presence I knew that if an individual didn't create a work presence, they would do things the way they thought was the way to do things. I recalled the concept of self-efficacy and how people would do what they believed they were best at. This concept might cause a disconnect between the individual and the department. Bob always talked about full engagement and that required focus and connection to the environment. I knew that without a work presence individuals would find ways to *get by* and this would create a less than optimum environment. I concluded that a lack of work presence that connected the virtual

64 VIRTUAL VIC: A MANAGEMENT FABLE

employee to the rest of the department could cause frustration and potential rework, thus slowing down the tasks being worked on.

With these conclusions I realized that I could create a TIP scale to measure the levels of trust, isolation, and presence. With this, every individual could monitor the current level of these human perceptions and in turn make themselves and the department the most productive. It would also be a way to have the constant monitoring tool that was needed in managing a blended workforce.

I made a simple triangle, each leg represented one of the three human perceptions. The strongest and most stable triangle is the equilateral. If all the sides are the same length, the relationship and the levels of trust, isolation, and presence would be in balance creating a strong and stable work situation. I wanted to make it easy to measure the human perceptions; therefore, each leg could be measured as a human perception on a scale of 1 to 10.

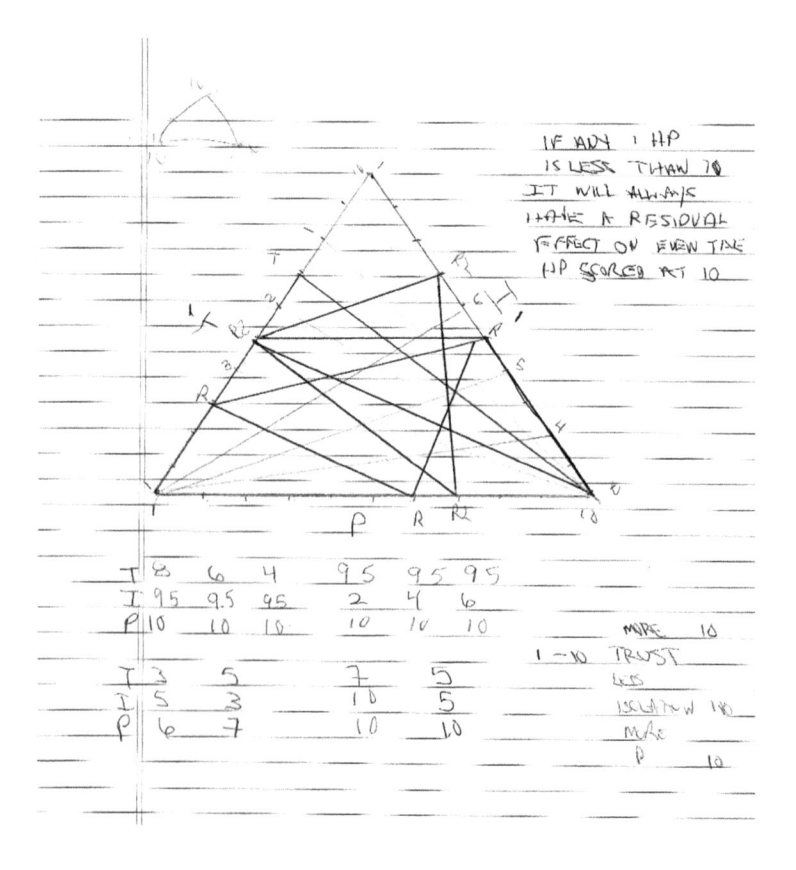

I could then ask questions to gain the level of each perception. Each score or level would translate to a length of that perception and once all three lines were established they could be used to create the triangle. For trust to be measured, one would have to respond to this question: How much trust do you have in yourself and the department? For isolation, how isolated do you feel and are you connected to the department? For presence, what is your level of work presence and engagement with the department related to department presence? By answering two humble questions, one about the individual and one about the department, the individual would understand their true fit in the department. I was conscious about not measuring the perception from just one lens. It was my premise that looking only at the individual level or the department could result in a false positive. For example, someone could feel very positive about their individual level of isolation, yet be disconnected from the department. If we measured the perception only from an individual level in this example, a person could score a 10 individually but score a 5 on the department level. The real score would therefore be a 7.5 versus a 10. The score of 7.5 is what we really needed to know to be a productive team. My hope was not to only gauge the individual level in seclusion but to get a true combined score since we had to function as a team, a department.

I also concluded that if any one perception were not at a 10, it would have a reducing effect on the other aspects regardless of how the individual scored on them. Every perception has a relationship and a correlation with the others. The triangle was the best for establishing the true strength of the human perceptions.

By getting the length of each line, score it 1–10 and making a triangle it would be easy to see the shape of the TIP scale triangle. The triangle's shape would be a visual reminder of the levels of trust, isolation, and presence currently perceived by each staff member. The six questions can be asked at any time and should be used to give the *in the moment* response of the human perceptions. This tool is designed to get the current status and be able to help head off long-term effects of a lack of trust, a feeling of isolation, and an absence of work presence.

For example, if someone had a low level of trust, that side would be shorter, causing the triangle to move away from the equilateral and move to a triangle that would be less stable, such as scalene. This might not mean that the relationship is completely in trouble but it would be a simple reminder that one of the perceptions is causing the triangle to be something other than the strongest, the equilateral.

I knew that I would introduce the TIP scale at my meeting and the department would implement it going forward as a tool that could be used between the individual and the manager or even among the full department.

I prepared the rest of my notes for my department meeting and was now ready to call my staff together and talk about all the lessons I had learned.

On the day of the meeting I was excited but also felt a level of anxiety hoping that my lessons would resonate with my staff.

I went to the office and welcomed my out-of-town staff as they arrived at the office. I had made arrangements for everyone to have a partner for the day's activities. I paired up staff and had them all sit in a U shape arrangement. The pairs would be seated side by side, and I would conduct my presentation by walking and talking while I was in the middle of the U.

As the meeting started I apologized for my mistakes—first and foremost, for not conducting a meeting on my first day. I told the staff that I would walk them through a series of stories and lessons I had learned about my approach in managing our blended team of colocated, part-time, and full-time virtual members.

I introduced the agenda and started to tell them about my lessons associated with trust. I told them about Reliable Reggie, who had opened my eyes to the aspects of trust. I explained how Reggie had told me I needed to ensure that my messages were clear and understood by all. I talked about the second meeting where I had vaguely set up the next day's meeting with Reggie without confirming his availability. I told them how Reggie provided clarity about how my first e-mail might not have been clear as to my expectations and how I drew wrong conclusions about the staff and their responses. I even laughed when I told them about the director of human resources not responding and the silly thought I had about what could be more important. After all, she was the director of

THE DEPARTMENT MEETING

human resources and most likely focused on the people she was serving and not responding to an unclear e-mail from her new manager. I finished my discussion about trust with telling each of them the awesome responsibility they all had in measuring the level of trust all the time. I told them about how the ugly stepbrother, distrust, could happen with broken commitments, unclear communications and to always be open and look for the opportunity to restate their positions.

I next talked about Solitary Samantha and how I learned that a once very productive employee lost her confidence because she began to feel isolated. I told them about how judging events by only their own view could cause others to feel isolated. I told them that they all needed to make sure that new policies and procedures were effectively communicated and understood by all before they could be fully implemented. Finally, I told them about how hard messages need to be communicated openly and timely. If there were going to be changes, they had to be discussed as soon as they were known to one individual and to ensure they were known to all.

When I moved to the topic of presence I thought maybe it would be best to ask a question. I asked the group to talk with their partner and share with them things that they had done in their individual work space and how they felt about it. In doing this exercise I wanted them to feel connected to their work space, where they spend their workday, and talk about it. I recalled how Bob made his staff feel connected to the new store by hanging pictures of the older store. After a few minutes I stopped the exercise and asked them all to recall how they felt about talking about their work presence. If they experienced a strong feeling of pride and connection, they knew what having presence was about. If they didn't feel that special connection, I challenged them to find someone who did and talk about it during a break. The important thing I concluded about presence is to really find the connection to the environment and remain committed, engaged. I told them being present was an important aspect of being able to truly understand the real awareness of their environment; by doing so they could be most productive.

I then explained about the TIP scale and opened the meeting for questions. After a few questions about how trust, isolation, and presence were part of not only the VWE but could be translated to the more traditional one, I was ready to conclude the meeting and get started with the new beginning.

I thanked everyone for attending the meeting and for all of their support as I struggled through the first few weeks on the job. I confirmed that I was fully committed to their success and would do what I could to make sure they were individually and as a department very successful by being a productive unit.

Finally, I had to admit that I had learned a very important lesson about leading. I learned what you often think coming into a situation might not be exactly what it ends up being. I had to be willing to self-reflect and look for alternative ways rather than holding onto my original thoughts and approach. I had come into my new job thinking that I could rely heavily on technology to make everyone's work life easier, including mine. I thought my staff and myself would be available around the clock with access to everything they needed 24 hours a day and this would make things easier and clearer. I thought how great it would be to give everyone freedom to balance their time and how not having everyone in the office was a money saver for the company and would not erode productivity.

What I ended up finding out was that nothing can replace the human touch and the human perceptions that go along with it. Technology needs to be used as a tool and not a crutch or a reason not to connect directly with individuals; otherwise, it can separate people and allow them to hide behind the machines and screens that are used. I concluded that even though there was cost saving related to working remotely, regular and dedicated face-to-face meetings were essential to having a productive work environment. I also knew that just being available through the use of technology was not all about being present in the moment and that at times being available around the clock was actually more of a distraction then a focused effort.

I knew that the VWE was a good thing. I knew that it was how organizations would continue to structure themselves. I was pleased I was finding ways to make the VWE more successful. I also knew that it could not function without being guided by the humans behind the actual work and just because you had a work–life balance doesn't mean that your work environment is really stable and balanced.

I sat at my desk as I did a few weeks prior. Instead of reading a note about how to log on to my new computer and drafting an e-mail to my staff, I took out a pen and paper. I asked myself the six questions about trust, isolation, and presence; determined the level of each; and used the TIP scale. Today, I scored a strong equilateral triangle; a few weeks ago I would have had a different picture. I reflected on my new sketch of a perfect equilateral triangle. This sketch was my moment in time to realize I now knew how to manage in the VWE.

I turned to look at my computer and found notes from each of my staff thanking me for the open discussion and productive department meeting. Each mentioned how excited they were toward becoming a productive unit. I knew then that I had come a long way.

CHAPTER 6
Self-Efficacy

The concept of self-efficacy was introduced in this book for a very important reason. Self-efficacy was part of the theory developed by Albert Bandura. Bandura explained in his theory that people have always strived to control the events within their lives.[1] By trying to control their lives, people are prone to do what they believe they are good at doing. There is no better feeling than doing something that is done well and knowing you have the skill to do it. This concept often comes into play when there are changes or challenges that require people to perform a task.

The VWE brings both changes and challenges to people working in this new environment. It is hard to imagine that the aspect of working away from the traditional work environment is not a change. It is even harder to imagine that with this remoteness associated with the VWE people are not challenged in terms of being productive.

It is an often-heard conversation that people who work virtually are actually working longer hours and being more productive because they lack the distractions of the other employees or activities that take place in a colocated work situation. This can be translated to a model that says a person starts their work process and their traditional behavior associated with work which results in an outcome for them. It is the outcome that matters in terms of productivity.

The person, the virtual worker, behaves in a particular way to achieve an outcome. This is where the concept of self-efficacy plays an integral part in the VWE. If the virtual workers are disconnected from the rest of the department, is their outcome in line with the expectations of the department or leader?

---

[1] A Bandura. 1997. *Self-Efficacy: The Exercise of Control* (New York, NY: W. H. Freeman and Company), p. i.

Since self-efficacy is about a person doing what they can control, it is very much possible that the virtual worker does what they believe is in their control. As the separation becomes longer and the disconnect increases, do the virtual workers start to do what they can control rather than what the department needs? Factors that are defined as human perceptions of trust, isolation, and presence, all play a critical force to the personal control element.

Work is a very large part of a person's everyday life. This provides them with a sense of self-worth. If a virtual worker's self-worth is challenged by the work structure, meaning they lack trust, feel isolated, or have a lack of work presence, their self-worth could be decreased. It, therefore, is logical that the individual worker will desire to increase their self-worth. The concept of self-efficacy plays an important role in the level of one's self-worth. By doing what a person believes they are good at, they can control the outcome. They will perform activities associated with this aspect. Increasing one's self-worth by doing a better job, having strong behaviors that they control might cause a disconnect with the department's mission. This causes more of a separation through missed expectations.

The more an individual controls their own environment, thus increasing their self-efficacy, the more they actually might become less productive to the greater good of the department even though they believe they are being more productive.

This can be seen in the amount of rework that is required by virtual workers. It can manifest itself in a way that requires the virtual workers to deliver less then optimal results to the department or can even require the virtual worker to work longer hours to achieve the needed results.

Leaders managing a blended workforce or only virtual workers need to be aware of how self-efficacy could have a negative result related to the productivity of these workers. It is paramount that the assumption of a virtual worker working longer hours is not translated to more productivity. The concept of self-efficacy has to be measured as does the level of trust, isolation, and presence that the virtual worker feels.

CHAPTER 7

Trust

The human perception of trust is part of this book as it a key element in the overall theory presented in the book, *The Human Side of Virtual Work: Managing Trust, Isolation, and Presence*. Trust is a human perception that has multiple layers. The depth of an individual feeling of trust is created by the person's belief that trust is present in their relationship or situation. This feeling of trust is often a one-way street but for it to be measured truthfully, it must be measured in terms of the relationship.

A person can have a high or low level of trust in a relationship but the other person in that relationship could have the opposite level. This is why trust has to be measured from both sides to establish a true level of the trusting relationship.

We might see this in the VWE where a virtual worker might feel a high level of trust, yet the other workers might not. This can happen for a variety of reasons. As discussed in the chapter on self-efficacy, a virtual worker might be working very hard and putting in long hours and believe that is creating a high level of trust. However, if the tasks being delivered to the department don't meet the expectations of the others, they in turn will lose trust toward the virtual worker.

Trust is a foundational aspect of human interaction. Individuals are often connected to their departments in terms of commitments. This is where trust plays a big part. This connection is more important in the VWE because there is a dependency to expect trust from all department members. In the example provided, the virtual worker believes they are connected and delivering a commitment, while the other workers believe the virtual worker failed to deliver the commitment required.

This creates the opposite effects desired by both parties. What actually happens is distrust. This is the evil stepbrother of trust. Trust and distrust are at the complete opposite ends of the trust spectrum. Morton Deutsch studied the aspects of distrust through his studies of social conflict.

There is no better example to illustrate this concept of trust and distrust than to use Deutsch's prisoner's dilemma game. In this game individuals were challenged to maximize their personal benefit by voting with or against other players.

The main element of the game is does a person think the other person will go along with their position so both players will reap a benefit at a lower level, yet both benefit, or will they choose to go on their own to maximize their own benefit, while risking everything?

Trust for the virtual workers has to come in the many different levels that trust can occur. Self-trust, kin to self-efficacy: Here the individual has to trust themselves to be able to perform the task and do what they believe they can accomplish with a high level of success. In other words, can they control the outcome?

Organizational trust: Do they trust the organization and does the organization trust them? This often manifests itself in effectiveness. Is the virtual worker being seen as effective in the duties and completion of tasks? As discussed, there could be a disconnect associated with this level of trust because the virtual worker believes they are being effective but the organization might see it otherwise; remember what happened to Samantha?

Individual trust: This is most often seen in terms of character, being a sincere person, having high ethics and integrity. Again, the problem here is do both people involved in the relationship feel the same degree of trust?

The VWE is ripe for each and every level of trust discussed to be challenged.

Leaders in the VWE must be vigilant about the human perception of trust and must ensure that it is measured and evaluated on a regular basis. It goes without saying that trust can take a long time to develop with many events needed to be tested for trust to form; unfortunately, trust can be destroyed quickly, and it is in the best interest of the organization to watch for events that can lead to the erosion of trust.

CHAPTER 8
Isolation

Isolation and the VWE go hand in hand. The fact that a person works remote from their main work location is the basis for isolation. As discussed, these human perceptions are not by the very nature negative; however, left unrecognized or unattended, they can turn negative. Isolation is a prime example of this effect. When an individual is left alone, they can become isolated.

Isolation is about being alone, apart, and separated from others. The individual might lack a connection with others. Isolation for humans is based on the individual's interpretation. How the individual interprets their sense of aloneness, connection, or attachment is critical to the level of isolation.

The fact of being separated is not by itself the perception of isolation, rather it is the individual's sense associated with the separation that matters. Like trust, isolation works on a continuum, from high to low. A person can feel isolated even when they are physically next to others, just as a person who is distant from others can have no feeling of isolation.

In the VWE the aspect of isolation can be defined in terms of the individual's sense of separation. If the individual feels separated and lonely, that will be interpreted as a high sense of isolation. This would be a score of 10 on the TIP scale.

It is reasonable to expect isolation is created by the structure of the VWE. The separation in terms of location needs to be managed so that the separation does not develop into a sense of high isolation, pulling the virtual worker into a negative perception. There are many studies on the effects of long-term isolation on people.[1,2] These studies explore

---

[1] House, J.S. 2001. "Social Isolation Kills But How and Why?" *Psychosomatic Medicine* 63 no. 2, pp. 273–276.

[2] DeVries, A.C., K. Karelina, J.S. Morris, G.J. Norman, H. Peng, and N. Zhang. 2009. "Social Isolation Alters Neuroninflammatory Response to Stroke." *Proceedings of the National Academy of Sciences of the United States of America* 1, pp. 1–15.

and explain the negative effects of isolation. These effects all tend to drive a person into a less productive individual for the group they are isolated from.

There are several forms of isolation that can arise in the VWE. There can be organizational isolation, which is twofold. As discussed, isolation is an individual's interpretation, yet in organizational isolation, not only is the individual measuring their sense of connection to the organization but also how the organization interacts towards and with the individual. We saw how Samantha felt isolated and started to pull away from her company, and we also saw her company start to pull away from her. This began the death spiral that ended with Samantha losing her job.

Social isolation is another form of isolation that can occur with the VWE. In this form the virtual worker lacks the connection to the others by way of social interactions. The adage of "Out of site out of mind" is what I am addressing here. The more the colocated workers plan and do things together, the more the virtual worker feels socially isolated. The local norms and behaviors are not understood by the virtual worker, and therefore, the level of social isolation increases.

Finally, there is the form of individual isolation. This isolation is developed by the individual and how they interpret their connection to their surroundings. This relates to how an individual feels in terms of normalcy. When we feel isolated, we feel out of sorts; we lack the sense of normal. When we feel a lack of normalcy, we strive to find it however and wherever we can. Often this is by acting in a way that gives control back to ourselves (see the self-efficacy chapter). This, as we have discussed, is another spiral that spins to create more isolation. Individuals, by taking control of their surroundings, tend to pull away from others who they believe have isolated them. This loop or spiral often increases the effect of isolation rather than curbing the original effect of it.

The bottom line when it comes to isolation is that in any form it can create a negative result. That negative result creates autonomy. Increased autonomy is in fact the pulling away from the group and acting alone. Autonomy by itself is not bad as it can be very empowering; however, in a blended team, the results are team oriented and not necessarily individual based. This can cause a less than productive team and add stress to the overall team. Leaders need to be focused on the balance between empowered autonomy and the negative side of isolation. Isolation left unattended can cripple both the individual and the organization.

CHAPTER 9

Presence

Presence is the third human perception (after trust and isolation) that is part of this book and theory that has been part of my research and studies. Like the other human perceptions this is also perceived on a continuum. I have defined presence with the concept of work presence to make the point clearer as it relates to the VWE.

There is an important aspect of the presence I am addressing in this book. There is a physical presence and there is the concept of feeling present. The difference is that just being physically present does not fully address the human perception of presence. The human perception of presence deals with the individual interpretation of being present whether colocated or not. Feeling present is feeling a connection related to one's surroundings. Recall the brief discussion in Bob's chapter about personal presence.

For virtual workers to be productive they must have a level of work presence that keeps them connected to the organization. Virtual workers must not distance themselves from their coworkers and organization and rely solely on their own surroundings.

A short description of the types of presence is provided to help illustrate how presence manifests itself at work:

- Environmental presence: It is the extent to which the environment itself recognizes and reacts to the person.
- Personal presence: It is the extent to which the person feels physically present in the environment.
- Social presence: It is the extent to which the person has the feeling of being together and communicating with others to achieve meaningful interactions, establish and maintain relations, and create productive social systems in each environment.

Each type of presence just presented can affect how an individual connects with their surroundings, and thus the work environment. Like trust and isolation, presence needs to be measured on a regular basis. Presence left to develop individually can have a negative result for the individual and the organization.

Creating a Work Presence

When individuals create a work presence for themselves they do so in a variety of ways. Some may do so to feel more comfortable with their personal sense of self. Some may define an individualized work schedule to differentiate between work and home life. The concept of making an individualized work environment might be a way for people who need to have the right work mind-set help establish some level of defining it is time to work. Some individuals might set rules about working. Some would get dressed as if they were going to work, take a lunch, and clock out at the end of the day. Some change their informal and formal business clothes to establish a sense of work and nonwork activity. The bottom line when it comes to presence in the work environment is clear: It has to be what the individual does associate with getting work done.

As will all the perceptions discussed in this book, to get the best out of people we need to find ways to maximize their efforts. Helping virtual workers establish a strong level of work presence will help with this maximization. Leaders must ensure that virtual workers feel present even when they are separated by distance. To feel a strong level of presence is to be a productive part of any team, department, or organization.

CHAPTER 10

Personal Touch

While I was finishing this book, I had a very sad event happen in my life: I lost my dear mother. She was a wonderful person and taught me and my brother and sister so many lessons while she was with us. Even on her deathbed she helped me with yet another lesson. This one was on point to helping me with my constant pursuit of the virtual world and the use of technology. She would often tell me the stories that she would come across that discussed how technology and the virtual world created challenges with social connection, trust, isolation, and presence. Truth be told, she often found ways to tie my field of study to these reports.

I have often been challenged with the use of technology as a way to replace the richness of direct, face-to-face, real connections. As I put my thoughts together about how to write about the human perceptions and the VWE that I have studied about, there was and always will be the trade-off between using technology as a crutch and using it as a convenient way to communicate and say things that most likely would not be said face-to-face. It provides a way to say things to others that are mean spirited; it is a way to yell at someone without the immediate repercussions, and as we have unfortunately seen, it is a way to bully others. All of these actions have a negative effect on the parties participating. My mom and I often talked about this. My mother grew up in a time when technology was not available as it is today. She would often comment on the way people communicated and say, what is wrong that people don't talk face-to-face anymore to solve their problems?

When she grew up and raised her family there was no Facebook, Twitter, instant messaging, Skype, or any other way to communicate to each other than by sitting down and talking it out face-to-face. We had many family discussions at the dinner table when we all sat together and talked about what was going on in our lives. She, like many of her generation, also had a strong sense of pride where family matters were discussed in the family circle and not shared publicly with the use of the aforementioned technology. We discussed the pros and cons of "this new way of sharing personal information" that she considered private.

When my brother called unexpectedly to say that my mother had been rushed to the hospital, there was no way to get my immediate family to Virginia, where she was located. When my wife and I arrived at the hospital and found out that she was terminally ill and would most likely not make it through the night, we were shocked. What do we do? How do we tell our children that their grandmother would be gone within hours and there was no way they could see her again? With my daughter in Japan with her husband, who was severing in the military, and my son in South Carolina, which put him seven hours away, how would they say goodbye? Of course, there was the phone that they could use but now they could also use FaceTime. Not only did technology allow them to talk to their grandmother before she passed away, they were able to see her and I believe, most importantly, that she was able to see them. She smiled so sweetly as she talked and watched each of them tell her how much they loved her. Even while she had to deal with death knocking at her door being able to see her grandchildren through the use of technology was a very special gift. I do wonder what the feeling would have been without the ability to see each other and only talk. This is when the lesson of using technology not as a crutch but as a tool to help people experience as close to the real situation as possible came to light. She was showing me and ultimately giving me her final OK and understanding that she supported this new way.

As we stood around her while she prepared to pass on, we as a family used technology to give my children an opportunity to be with her and the rest of the family. We called both my daughter and my son and for the next several hours up to her taking her last breath they were there with her and us. We used FaceTime to allow them to share in the many stories that were told that day. They laughed with us, listened to the songs we played for her, and prayed with us during her final hours. They were there even though they were not physically with us. My mother got to see them, talk to them, and tell them how she felt while they were able to do the same.

This was a beautiful situation and it is how technology is supposed to be used. It is supposed to help fill the gaps that exist in a world that places family in many different locations.

We were able to use technology to bring my family together when time and space would not allow it otherwise. We were not using technology at the table where we all sat to eat dinner together. We were not texting each other while we were in the same house just rooms apart. We were not using it as we drove distracted by it, or while we were out to dinner at a restaurant rather than talking to the people we were out to dinner with. We used it on this day to bring us together not to separate us.

As always, my mom had a lesson for me and the rest of the family: Use technology to connect and make the bonds of relationships stronger. Don't use technology to hide behind developing real relationships and always believe that a strong relationship will take honest work. My mom showed us that day, her last day on this earth, to never lose or forget the power of the human touch.

Endnotes

This book has presented a fable about Virtual Vic, who learned lessons from his informal board of directors (BOD), Reliable Reggie, Solitary Samantha, and Being Bob. This book did not get into a lot of theory and research related to either the virtual work environment (VWE) or the three human perceptions of trust, isolation, and presence. There are many books that can get into great detail on these topics. My book *The Human Side of Virtual Work: Managing Trust, Isolation, and Presence* goes into greater detail on these topics. It was by design that created in a story format the aspects that affect all individuals associated with the VWE as I believe it is through this story that the challenges associated with the VWE can best be understood and reflected upon.

I encourage anyone working in the VWE to dig deeper into any of the situations that they related to in Vic's story. I am hopeful that over time the concepts discussed will become nonexistent in the VWE and this new structure does indeed make all departments productive units and keep alive the human touch.

About the Author

Laurence M. Rose (Larry) has been an executive leader for the past 16 years. He has more than 30 years of government and commercial business and operational experience. He has worked with large, medium, and small federal contractors and has been managing virtual teams at all levels. He has operated his own business for over 30 years and is seen by many as an entrepreneur. His dissertation explored the human side of the virtual work environment. He has taught classes at the business level in topics of contracts management, negotiations, and program management. He has been recognized for his outstanding presentation style and approach to teaching.

Index

Assumption, 23
ATM, 9
Autonomy, 76

Bandura, Albert, 71
Board of directors (BOD)
　informal, 61–62
　personal, 61
Bob, 47–59, 61–62, 68

Castaway (movie), 32
Colocated employees, 25, 27, 30, 33–34, 41, 49, 76
Commitment, unspoken, 23

Department meeting, 61–69
　agenda of, 62
　planning, 62
　structure of, 62–63
　TIP scale, 63–69
Deutsch, Morton, 74
Dilemma game, 74
Distrust, 63, 73–74
Dropbox, 2

E-mail, 7–10, 34
Employees, connecting with work environment, 54–55
Environmental presence, 79

Face-to-face interactions, 26–27
FaceTime, 82
Feeling present, 79
Ford, Henry, 30

Gandhi, 30
GPS, 4, 6

Human perceptions
　isolation. *See* Isolation
　presence. *See* Presence
　trust. *See* Trust

Human resources (HR), 9
Human touch, 3, 5, 34, 44, 69
　power of, 81–83

Individual isolation, 76
Individual trust, 74
iPad, 2, 7
Isolation, 29–44, 63, 68, 75–76
　to gain level of, 65

Leadership, 8, 27, 29
Loneliness, 4

Meeting. *See* Department meeting

No-win situation, 37

One-on-one conversation, 33
Organizational isolation, 76
Organizational trust, 74

Pay Per View (movie), 11
Personal presence, 62, 79
Physical presence, 79
Presence, 47–59, 63–68, 79–80.
　See also specific Presence

Reggie, 15–28, 47–48, 61–62, 66

Samantha, 29–44, 47–48, 61–62, 68
Sarbanes–Oxley Act, 20
Schein, Edgar, 48
Self-belief, 30
Self-conscience, 40
Self-doubt, 40
Self-efficacy, 30, 49, 63, 71–72
Self-trust, 74
Self-worth, 72
Shared learning, 38
Shared responsibility, 38
Skype, 34
Smartphone, 3

Social isolation, 76
Social learning theory, 38, 63
Social presence, 79

Technology
 to connect and stronger relationships, 81–83
 use of, 1–12, 69
Text message, 11, 12
Traditional work environment, 34, 44
Trust, 15–28, 63, 66–67, 73–74. *See also specific Trusts*
 communicating well-defined expectations and established goals, 23–26
 effective communication, 26–27
 to gain level of, 65
 unspoken commitment, 23
Trust, isolation and presence (TIP) scale, 63–69

Virtual employees, 7, 10, 33–34, 37, 44
Virtual work environment (VWE), 16, 35, 48
 no-win situation, 37
Voicemail messages, 34

Wi-Fi, 2
Work presence, 63–64
 creating, 80
 elements associated with, 52, 55–56
Work–life balance, 8, 35, 48, 69

OTHER TITLES IN THE HUMAN RESOURCE MANAGEMENT AND ORGANIZATIONAL BEHAVIOR COLLECTION

- *Skilling India: Challenges and Opportunities* by S. Nayana Tara and Sanath Kumar
- *Redefining Competency Based Education: Competence for Life* by Nina Morel and Bruce Griffiths
- *No Dumbing Down: A No-Nonsense Guide for CEOs on Organization Growth* by Karen D. Walker
- *From Behind the Desk to the Front of the Stage: How to Enhance Your Presentation Skills* by David Worsfold
- *Creating a Successful Consulting Practice* by Gary W. Randazzo
- *How Successful Engineers Become Great Business Leaders* by Paul Rulkens
- *Leading the High-Performing Company: A Transformational Guide to Growing Your Business and Outperforming Your Competition* by Heidi Pozzo
- *The Concise Coaching Handbook: How to Coach Yourself and Others to Get Business Results* by Elizabeth Dickinson
- *Lead Self First Before Leading Others: A Life Planning Resource* by Stephen K. Hacker
- *The How of Leadership: Inspire People to Achieve Extraordinary Results* by Maxwell Ubah
- *Managing Organizational Change: The Measurable Benefits of Applied iOCM* by Linda C. Mattingly
- *Creating the Accountability Culture: The Science of Life Changing Leadership* by Yvonnne Thompson
- *Conflict and Leadership: How to Harness the Power of Conflict to Create Better Leaders and Build Thriving Teams* by Christian Muntean
- *Precision Recruitment Skills: How to Find the Right Person For the Right Job, the First Time* by Rod Matthews

Announcing the Business Expert Press Digital Library

Concise e-books business students need for classroom and research

This book can also be purchased in an e-book collection by your library as

- a one-time purchase,
- that is owned forever,
- allows for simultaneous readers,
- has no restrictions on printing, and
- can be downloaded as PDFs from within the library community.

Our digital library collections are a great solution to beat the rising cost of textbooks. E-books can be loaded into their course management systems or onto students' e-book readers.
The **Business Expert Press** digital libraries are very affordable, with no obligation to buy in future years. For more information, please visit **www.businessexpertpress.com/librarians**. To set up a trial in the United States, please email **sales@businessexpertpress.com**.